BALLET IN RUSSIA

A HISTORY OF
BALLET IN RUSSIA
(1613–1881)

By
CYRIL W. BEAUMONT
with a Preface by
ANDRÉ LEVINSON

ILLUSTRATED

LONDON
C. W. BEAUMONT
75, Charing Cross Road, W.C.2
1930

First published in 1930

This edition published by:

The Noverre Press
Southwold House
Isington Road
Binsted
Hampshire
GU34 4PH

© 2020 The Noverre Press

ISBN 978-1-906930-89-2

To
ANDRÉ LEVINSON
IN FRIENDSHIP AND ADMIRATION

INTRODUCTION

IT has afforded me much pleasure to be invited to contribute a few pages of introduction to Mr. Cyril W. Beaumont's book, in which will be found assembled and explained innumerable facts regarding the origin and history of ballet in Russia. In the first place, the author must be congratulated on the judicious selection he has displayed in dealing with so great a subject. Already this scholar, who both understands the technique of dancing and is a man of taste, has earned well of the Dance; his model translations and faithful reprints of old masters of choregraphy, his patient bibliographical researches, his manuals, summarising with insight and precision the principles of classic training according to the method of Maestro Cecchetti, constitute a whole worthy of admiration and without parallel in other countries, and form a library for both dance-lover and dancer. But never was a publication more opportune than that of this detailed history, in which the author has marshalled, day by day, a host of documents and notes, *scenarii*, biographies, critical accounts and poetic compliments, dates and figures, casts of important first nights, and a mass of other information. And on this framework of authentic fact he has embroidered a thousand arabesques: those anecdotes and legends which make the undercurrents of history so delightful because they depict so admirably an epoch and its setting, the inimitable picturesqueness and atmosphere peculiar to the former Imperial Theatres of Russia.

Mr. Beaumont has had the happy thought to base his book for the most part (he himself makes this acknowledgment) on the valuable work of M. Alexis Pleschayev, the kindly doyen of Russian *balletomanes*, who was a witness of the most glorious days of the Maryinsky Theatre. That the picture of Russian dancing may be complete, Mr

Beaumont should issue a second volume, a compilation as able and delectable as this, devoted to the company attached to the Grand Theatre at Moscow; because there has always existed between these two capitals of Russian ballet the same rivalry and difference in style. As for the St. Petersburg ballet, we see it come to life again, thanks to Mr. Beaumont's book, in all the fairy splendour of its former days, here so faithfully depicted.

* * *

From among a multitude of particulars there emerge the main lines of the evolution of a style. We shall endeavour to retrace the whole of its sweeping curve. And, in doing so, we shall discover that, in collecting materials for a history of ballet in Russia, the author adds an important chapter to that of the artistic affinities between Western Europe and Russia. A French dancing-master in the reign of the Empress Elizabeth was the first to establish a regular troupe of dancers and organise its training. The Emperor Paul sent for Le Picq, the best pupil of the *chorégraphe* Noverre, restorer and theorist of the *ballet d'action*; and his successor, Alexander I, published, at his own expense, the master's literary works. Later, he engaged the famous Didelot, prodigious as a dancer, but ugly and almost deformed; the "flying ballets" of that gnome-like genius triumphed at both Court and Capital. As a teacher, he created a whole generation of Russian dancers, including the famous Istomina, whom the national poet Pushkin describes to us as "light as down blown by Æolus." He also sent for Duport, the fortunate rival of the declining Vestris, and the fabulous fees demanded by the great dancer became, like his amorous adventures, the favourite topic of conversation in the drawing-rooms of the two Russian capitals. Didelot, who, moreover, knew how to adapt himself to the tastes of his second country, and went so far as to take the theme of his ballet, *The Captive of the Caucasus*, from a celebrated Russian poem, was thus adopted by Russia. His destiny resembled that of an architect such as Thomas de Thomon, or that of a sculptor such as Falconet. Overwhelmed with tribulations by the dictators of the Paris Opéra, ejected by Pierre Gardel, this French master would have pined away in some provincial theatre. Russia took him, cared for him, allowed him to prove his worth. The wealthy patronage of Russian monarchs and noblemen was a providential help for Western geniuses.

French and Italian artists, builders and dancers, let themselves be carried away by the grandeur of Imperial pomp, by the unprecedented scale in which all enterprises were conceived in that virgin land; they could conform the extent of their dreams to the immensity of the Russian plain. Thomon could build a monumental Exchange resembling the Temple of Pæstum, Falconet could hew out of solid granite the incurving base of his monument to Peter the Great—the bronze horseman. So Russia became the refuge of the slighted. This elective affinity with French dancers manifested itself particularly at St. Petersburg, the window overlooking Europe. If the legendary shooting-stars, the Taglionis and Elsslers, always on the road between the San Carlo Theatre of Naples and the Doric pediment of the Grand Theatre of Moscow, came to gather new laurels in the "Northern Palmyra," French masters played an even more effective part by virtue of their continuity.

There, Titus, who succeeded Didelot, produced *La Sylphide*. There, good old Pluque collaborated with Jules Perrot the Aerial, whose *Esmeralda*, a choregraphic paraphrase from Victor Hugo's novel, still has its place in the repertory of the Academic Theatres of Leningrad, the capital which changed its name and was afterwards deprived of its royalty. *Esmeralda*, however, is by no means the oldest of the French ballets which survive on the Russian stage; *La Fille Mal Gardée*, which Dauberval conceived about 1760, still retains its first bloom; Anna Pavlova, in reviving this gem of old France, continues the tradition of the Maryinsky Theatre, and Théophile Gautier's *Giselle* is still the favourite with Northern "stars." The Russian ballet, however, had completely neglected popular legend, from which source of inspiration springs choregraphic folklore, the rites and ceremonies of rustic life, the games and round-dances of village youth, whose rules go back to the Pagan Age. Once more a French master endeavoured to bridge this gap. Saint-Léon produced a ballet based on the popular tale, *The Little Hump-backed Horse*, versified by Erchov. Three worlds confront and penetrate one another in that comical fairyland; first, the manners of the Russian *mujik*, his squatting dances in birch-bark shoes, the samovar, the knout; then an Orient in the manner of an *image d'Epinal*; and, superimposed on these two visions, the ideal kingdom of the classic dance. An altogether conventional production in an imitation Russian style, the "star" with the *kokoshnik* —Muscovite diadem—on her head, and wearing satin shoes and tartalan *tutu*! Slav musical themes accented by the *taqueté* of *pointes*! But it cleared the way for future ballets like *Petrouchka* or *L'Oiseau de Feu*. No one, however, so well embodied the reciprocal penetration of Western style and popular tradition as the late Mme. Sobietchanska of the Moscow ballet, a pupil of Carlo Blasis, the Milanese master, in her Russian dance in heeled shoes, which Mme. Geltser introduced to the Parisian public some twenty years ago. And it is but eight years since the artistes of the former Imperial Theatres, disguised as Academic Theatres, but faithful to their past, celebrated with splendour the centenary of him who had definitely established the Russian ballet in all its glory. Now this great Russian, so justly venerated, was a Frenchman again. It had devolved on Marius Petipa to "colonise" Russia by importing into it the ideas of his motherland. It is well known that to-day the colony dominates the capital. Now Marius Petipa was borne to the Northern shore on the rising tide of Romanticism.

Since Petipa was French, the tradition he embodied was French. But in order that the new and magnificent blossoming of an art which languished on its native soil, the Paris Opéra, should come to full flower, it was imperative that it should be enriched, rejuvenated, stimulated by the fertile and youthful Slav blood, by the ecstatic ardour and ductile intelligence of Russian dancers, by conceptions as vast as the steppes which stretched far out of sight towards the Orient.

Again, Théophile Gautier, at the time of his travels

in Russia, in 1858, had remarked on the unparalleled cohesion of the *ensembles*, the homogeneity of a youthful and charming *corps de ballet* subjected to a unique training, forged by tradition, the " first in the world " in his opinion. And the author of *Emaux et Camées* had praised highly the importance of the Imperial School, an admirable centre of choregraphic education. However, despite the fortitude of an Andreyanova contending against Taglioni in *La Sylphide*, the victory remained with the foreign " stars " for half a century more. The vogue of the great Milanese *ballerine*, the Cornalbas, Zucchis, and Legnanis, sustained the reverberating quarrel between the two schools; the Italian, more *terre à terre*, exceeded the limits of technique in regard to *pointes* and *pirouettes*; the French strove for elegance and elevation in both the poetic and gymnastic senses of the word. This struggle, often indecisive (of which the famous journalist Skalkovsky was the witty historian), between mechanism and intellect, virtuosity and feeling, aided Russian dancers above all to realise their own value. At the beginning of the century the Russian became master in his own house. In a few years a prodigious line of Russian stars ousted their Milanese rivals. The Kshesinskayas, Pavlovas, Trefilovas and Preobrazhenskayas triumphed in the ballets of Tchaikovsky and Glazunov by combining the best of two schools and uniting exercise to poetry, and mime to pure dancing. The traditional style became regenerated, impregnated with feeling, rejuvenated by enthusiasm, exalted by reverie, without detriment to that grand air of nobility and that discreet reserve peculiar to Court Theatres.

Male dancing had been somewhat neglected through the reign of the eternal feminine. Men shone chiefly in " character," stylisations full of the brilliancy of traditional dances ; thus the Polish dynasty of the Kshesinskys was unrivalled in the mazurka. Others, such as Gerdt and the brothers Legat, were masters of mime and supported the " star " in *pas de deux*.

Michel Fokine, a dancer in the grand style and an ardent teacher, who recognised and formed the genius of Nijinsky, prepared a veritable renaissance of male dancing, the style which had predominated during the epoch of Vestris.

The Vladimirovs, Obukhovs and such like, whose reputations nowadays are world-wide, were his pupils. But ere long he subordinated his methods of training to his researches in choregraphy, which were to make his name famous. There, again, he founded a school. Boris Romanov followed Fokine's example as *maître de ballet* and excelled, moreover, in character dancing—wan Pierrrot or savage Polovtsian. At the same time Moscow mobilised its forces. The Moscow ballet was, indeed, directed by M. Gorsky, a rebellious pupil of Petipa, in a style differing from the haughty formalism and discreet elegance that prevailed at the Maryinsky Theatre; there, the primitive fury of the man of the steppes found full vent; the action was heightened by pathos, often to an extravagant degree; an unrestrained picturesqueness permeated the scenes and costumes of the famous Korovin; nevertheless, talent abounded. Mme. Geltser, already mentioned, was supported by Mlles. Balashova and Caralli, so different in their great beauty, and Sophia Fedorova, who mingled the vivacity of the gypsy singer with the tragedy of one of Dostoievsky's characters, and ever so many more whom I dare not mention in this brief review for fear of prolonging this list, or rather this "catalogue of heroines," to employ the language of Homer. But it is only fitting that I should call to mind the superb men, more athletic and more alert than those at St. Petersburg, save Volinin, that impeccable model of classicism: Mordkin, Novikov, Zhukov, Smoltzov.

With such resources, the supremacy of Russian ballet soon became incontestable. Yet again, an excess of vigour tormented the rejuvenated Russian ballet, fomented discord and revolt against the authority of the venerable Marius Petipa, and against that of Leon Ivanov, the most modest of geniuses, who had been thrust into the shade by the glory of the native of Marseille, but who, in collaboration with Tchaikovsky, had contrived *Le Casse-Noisette* and a part of *Le Lac des Cygnes*—marvels of choregraphy. An outlet for this feverish energy was imperative. And, for the good of the Imperial Theatres, it was flung at Europe, so soon to be conquered and charmed. The one who led that youthful band was Fokine, inspired by the example of Isadora Duncan, attentive to the recommendations of painters desirous of theatrical glory; he abhorred the fashions of yester-year and champed the bit. But a great will was necessary to lead to victory the Imperialism of Russian choregraphy, an Attila who was also a man of refined tastes, a crafty impresario who at the same time was a natural force. I refer to Serge de Diaghilev. In 1908 he launched the first assaulting wave. Two seasons later, Bakst's *Schéhérazade*, based on Rimsky-Korsakov's music, was acclaimed at Paris; this triumph gave birth to a whole new orientation in the decorative and sumptuary arts, its influence was even reflected in furniture, fashion, and ladies' dress. Some years later, Diaghilev, having already revealed Stravinsky's musical genius in *Petrouchka*, that pantomime in music, a complete masterpiece, realised with *Le Sacre de Printemps* the work that will dominate the musical inspiration of the epoch. All these successes were, more or less, due to the dancing. Indeed, the splendid onrush of the wave of Polovtsian hordes swept all before it. But the real nature of that art, hidden beneath exotic finery and barbaric paroxysm, was misunderstood. Under that disguise were manifested the virtues of a traditional school. Nijinsky, a feline negro in *Schéhérazade*, a tragic puppet in *Petrouchka*, did no more than carry on and crown the more than two centuries' old tradition of a Pécourt, transplanted to the most fertile of soils by the genius of Didelot and Petipa, impregnated with Slav vigour, augmented by a whole gamut of emotions, fragrant or fierce, but ever faithful to the vital principle which created it. These women, seraphic or furious, these superb young men, were all formed by exercise, admirably *placés, ouverts, allongés* and made supple by a classic training.

* * *

I perceive a little too late that my account has exceeded by half a century, the length of two generations, the period covered in Mr. Beaumont's book. But it only proves the more how right our author was to connect the "Ballets Russes," the famous, pre-eminently modern and cosmopolitan company, with the national tradition that survives in Russia, and in explaining the present by the past. The European public has witnessed in amazement the conquest of both the Old World and the New by Russian theatrical dancing. The historian, to whom we are indebted for this fine work, has shown us the penetration of Western manners into Russia and the slow gestation of Russian choregraphic genius.

ANDRÉ LEVINSON.

Paris, August 1st, 1930.

AUTHOR'S PREFACE

OF recent years few events have exercised so great an influence on the art of the theatre as the performances of ballet given by the late Diaghilev Company. But it is extremely doubtful whether this company could have been founded—setting aside all questions of success—without the splendid material borrowed from the Imperial Russian Ballet. The appreciation of that fact has naturally given rise to a demand for information regarding the origin and development of ballet in Russia, particularly by students of the Dance and those intending to make it their profession.

Since, at present, no book of the kind exists in the more familiar languages,[1] I have ventured to compile a short history which covers the period 1613 to the beginning of 1881, that is, from the accession of Alexis Mikhaylovich to the death of Alexander II. Even in the merest outline the history of ballet in Russia presents a fascinating and romantic story of incidents which could only happen in that mysterious country of strange people, whose most cultured representatives still bear in their veins traces of that barbaric strain which, when present in excess, produces a Peter the Great or a Lenin.

The principal sources of information are naturally Russian, a language of which my knowledge is strictly limited. This initial difficulty, however, was smoothed away by the kind and generous help of my friends, M. S. N. Trofimov and Mme. Korotkevich, who translated for me any material that I required. I am particularly indebted to the former who spent a great many evenings with me going through various Russian works which it was felt might afford information or clues to possible sources. I have also to thank Col. V. Korotkevich, C.B.E., the

[1] I except the gay sketches contained in P. d'Alheim's *Sur les Pointes*, Paris, 1897.

proprietor of the Russian Library at 32, Coptic Street, London, for his kindness in allowing me constant access to his collection.

My principal authority has been Alexander Pleshchayev's classic history of ballet in Russia—*Nash Balet*, first published in 1897, then reissued in an enlarged form in 1899; the references quoted are taken from the first edition. I have, as far as possible, compared Pleshchayev's statements with those of other writers and in the case of difference placed a note accordingly. As regards sources other than Russian, and, apart from literature directly concerned with the dance, I have gleaned a measure of interesting information from the extensive reading of English and French histories, biographies, and memoirs relating to Russia.

Since the average dance student is unfamiliar with Russian history, I have introduced into the text, at convenient intervals, a brief account of the sequence of events, to afford some idea of the prevailing conditions.

In the transliteration of Russian names, I have, in general, adopted the system advocated by Prince D. S. Mirsky in his *History of Russian Literature*. All names of ballets are given in their English equivalent, except where I considered them to be more familiar in their French titles; for instance: *Koniok Gorbunok* becomes *The Hump-backed Horse*, while *Deva Dunaya* is rendered as *La Fille du Danube*.

All dates referring to performances and so on given in Russia are in the " old style," and are thus eleven days behind our own calendar in the eighteenth century and twelve days behind in the nineteenth. All dates relating to events outside Russia are in the " new style."

In 1923, I contributed some preliminary articles on the history of ballet in Russia which appeared in *The Dancing World*. Much of the present work was published serially in *The Dance Journal*, since when it has been revised and enlarged.

CYRIL W. BEAUMONT

CONTENTS

PART		PAGE
I.	From the Accession of Michael Fedorovich to the Death of Theodore Mikhaylovich	1
II.	Under Peter the Great	7
III.	From the Accession of Catherine I. to the Death of Anne	12
IV.	From the Regency of Biron to the Death of Elizabeth	19
V.	From the Accession of Peter III. to the Death of Catherine II.	24
VI.	Under Paul I.	33
VII.	Under Alexander I.	38
VIII.	Under Nicholas I.	53
IX.	Under Alexander II.	85

ILLUSTRATIONS

	FACING PAGE
MASQUERADE GIVEN AT VIENNA IN 1698	4
A BALL FOR DWARVES DURING THE REIGN OF PETER THE GREAT	8
MASQUERADE DURING THE REIGN OF PETER THE GREAT	12
MASQUERADE GIVEN DURING THE REIGN OF ANNE	16
THE BOLSHOY THEATRE, ST. PETERSBURG—EARLY NINETEENTH CENTURY	36
IVAN VALBERG (LIESOGOROV)	40
CHARLES DIDELOT	40
MARIE TAGLIONI IN " LA FILLE DU DANUBE "	44
AVDOTIA ISTOMINA	46
EKATERINA TELESHOVA	46
OLGA SCHLEFOCHT	46
A TAGLIONI DAY AT THE BOLSHOY THEATRE	48
MARIE TAGLIONI IN " LA GITANE "	52
ELENA ANDREYANOVA	56
ELENA ANDREYANOVA: MEDAL STRUCK IN HER HONOUR	60
CHRISTIAN JOHANNSEN	64
LUCILE GRAHN	68
FANNY ELSSLER IN " LE DIABLE BOITEUX "	72
JULES PERROT AND CARLOTTA GRISI IN " ESMERALDA "	76
GALA PERFORMANCE AT PETERHOV ON JULY 11TH, 1851	80
MARTHA MURAVIEVA	84
FANNY CERRITO IN " ONDINE "	86

ILLUSTRATIONS

	FACING PAGE
Nadezhda Bogdanova	88
Amalia Ferraris in " Les Elfes "	92
Caroline Rosati in " Le Corsaire "	96
Marius Petipa in " La Fille du Pharaon "	100
Charles V. A. de Saint-Léon	104
Ekaterina Vazem	108
Nicholas Goltz	112
Evgenia Sokolova	116
Matilda Madaeva	120
Alexandra Prikhunova	124

PART I

FROM THE ACCESSION OF MICHAEL FEDOROVICH TO THE DEATH OF THEODORE MIKHAYLOVICH

(1613-1682)

THE first mention of dancing in Russia occurs in the reign of the first Romanov, the Tsar Michael Fedorovich (1613-1645), when we learn of the existence of national dances. There was also a tight-rope dancer[1] who gave lessons in dancing. Again, just as in the Italy of the fifteenth century, after the famous combined ballet and banquet given by Bergonzio di Botta in 1489, every petty prince aspired to possess his own troupe of dancers; so a century later in Moscow it is recorded that many notables, such as the Dolgoruky, the Sheremetev and the Golitsin, possessed their own companies of female dancers, probably slaves, who performed for their amusement. But these were not dancers in the sense of being trained executants, but rather buffoons; rude comedians who improvised movements to arouse the laughter of their audiences.

At the beginning of the seventeenth century, Russia was divided into two portions: the Tsardom of Moscovy, then the whole of the Russian Empire, which was Eastern Russia; and the Polish Republic and Lithuania, which comprised the whole of the immense plain lying between Kurland, Moldavia, the upper Desna and the Boug, and was governed nominally by a king, in reality by the *Sejm* or Diet, an assembly of nobles and gentlemen.

[1] Ivan Loduigui. He also taught drum-beating.

At the period under review, Moscovy was "an Empire of little villages," as she has been aptly described by a Russian historian. Trade was very difficult, owing to the bad roads and the great distances between the settlements. There were few markets and fairs. The great majority of the people were quite uneducated, and few noblemen could write their names. The people were profoundly religious and bigoted in the extreme. Nearly everything that contributed to pleasure or the enjoyment of life was regarded as a mortal sin; feasting and hunting, however, were regarded as pardonable indulgences. Custom was a god of immeasurable power; to alter the mode of dressing one's hair, or the accepted shape of a garment, was akin to being possessed by the Devil.

The Russian women were rated as of little value. Woman was regarded as an irresponsible being particularly susceptible to the temptations of the Devil. For this reason she was kept secluded within the walls of her *terem* (as the women's apartments were called), from which she emerged seldom, except to wait by order of her husband on his guests, or to proclaim his position by showing off the rich dresses he had thought fit to bestow upon her. The appalling ignorance, the bigotry, the state of semi-barbarity common to the majority of the inhabitants cannot be exaggerated. As for the Dance, a Russian chronicler has written: "When dancing and the strife of fiddles begin, the good angels flee away, as bees before smoke, and the Devil and his angels rejoice."

The foundation proper of the dance in Russia commenced in the reign of the Tsar Alexis Mikhaylovich (1645–1676). At this period there were resident in Moscow over 1,000 foreigners, who dwelt in a special portion of the town known as the *Nyemetskaya Sloboda* (German Quarter). The description "German" was applied to all foreigners, irrespective of their nationality. But the Russian people were very interested in the European community, and borrowed and introduced several of their customs, so that they should appear cultivated and well-educated in the eyes of the foreign embassies that from time to time came to Moscovy. An interest arose in the dramatic art, as a result of which all Russian ambassadors abroad were enjoined strictly to report fully on all performances of the kind which they witnessed.

Likhatchev (Moscovite Ambassador to the Court of Tuscany) greatly astonished his countrymen in 1660 with his account of what he had seen in Florence. He seems to have been particularly impressed by a theatrical performance given by the Duke of Tuscany, which he describes thus : " A hall appeared, and in this hall appeared a sea, waves rolled, and in the sea were fishes, and on the fishes men were riding, and at the top of this hall was a sky, and in the clouds men were sitting . . . and from the sky a grey-haired man in a chariot descended on a cloud, and opposite him in another chariot was a beautiful girl, and the horses of the chariots were quite alive, moving their legs. And the prince said that one was the Sun and the other the Moon. . . . And in another change of scene appeared about 50 men in half-armour, who began to fight with falchions and swords, and to shoot with harquebuses, and about 3 of them appeared to be killed. And a number of very wonderful youths and maidens came in front of a gold curtain, and performed many marvels."

Presently foreign customs were introduced into the houses of the Tsar and his boyars to soften the native roughness. There developed a liking for dramatic entertainments, and the Russian ambassadors abroad were directed to entice to Moscow the most accomplished trumpet players who could play the best dances. This decision was taken very timidly, because music was regarded as the amusement of the Devil—a " contamination of the soul.[1]"

The Tsar was greatly aided in his task of government by Athanasius Ordin-Nashchokin, who may be described as Russia's first diplomatist and statesman. He was succeeded by a still more remarkable personality, the boyar Artamon Sergeyevich Matveyev, who married a Scottish lady.[2] From her he became acquainted with European manners and customs. He furnished his house in European style,

---

[1] In 1649, by order of the Patriarch Joseph, all the musical instruments in Moscow—save only those that belonged to the Tsar's personal band—were seized and publicly burnt.

[2] Her maiden name was Hamilton.

and began to collect fine carpets, ingenious clocks, rare pictures and china.

On May 15th, 1672, Matveyev, in accordance with the Tsar's orders, instructed Count Von Staden to recruit in Kurland, Riga and other towns, all kinds "of good master workmen, together with very excellent skilled trumpeters, and masters who would know how to contrive plays." He returned from his mission in December, with but "one trumpeter" and "four musicians," the Germans almost everywhere having viewed the engagement with distrust, owing to the rumours circulated regarding the cruel treatment that might be meted out to them.

In the meantime, it would seem that the Tsar became impatient to see some kind of play acted at his Court, for, on June 4th, without waiting for Von Staden's return, he commanded Johann Gottfried Gregory, one of the Lutheran pastors residing in the German quarter, to celebrate the birth of the Tsarevich Peter by performing a play based on the biblical subject of Esther. It was to be given at the Tsar's country house at Preobrazhenskoe (a village near Moscow), and there, under Matveyev's directions, a large room was fitted up for the purpose. This primitive theatre was called the *Komidyeinnaya Khoromna*, or Hall of Comedy.

Pastor Gregory, in collaboration with some teachers in the German school, wrote a "tragi-comedy" styled *The Acts of Artaxerxes*. He then collected a company of sixty-four volunteer actors, mostly drawn from the better class of tradesfolk, and an orchestra. The latter was composed partly of foreigners from the *Nyemetskaya Sloboda* and partly of slaves from Matveyev's household. The actual performance—said to have occupied ten hours—was given on October 17th, 1672, and met with much appreciation, while the Tsar generously rewarded all those who had taken part in the representation.

Encouraged by this success, Gregory produced a number of other plays written by himself or in collaboration with others—*Tobias, The Chaste Joseph, Adam and Eve*, and *How Judith cut off the Head of Holofernes*. The last is of particular interest, for it is generally regarded as the *first Russian opera*; it contained seven acts, divided into twenty-nine

MASQUERADE GIVEN AT VIENNA IN 1698
in honour of the Russian Embassy

scenes, and over sixty characters—all the female parts were taken by youths. Notwithstanding their biblical themes, these were not Mystery Plays after the mediæval manner, but plays of an entirely new kind, which astonished the audiences by their awful scenes of execution, combats, and firing of harquebuses. There was a comic element provided by a jester, whose performance often exceeded the bounds of decency. The Russians now wished to develop their native talent, and, in 1673, Gregory taught the theatrical art to twenty-six youths of native birth who were henceforth to be known as "the Comedians of His Majesty the Tsar."

In this same year[1] a *divertissement* was performed for the first time; it was presented as a prologue to a play. The *divertissement*, entitled *Orpheus*, was arranged by Heinrich Schütz. It was an imitation of *Orpheus and Eurydice*, devised by a Wittenberg professor, A. Büchner, which was given in 1638 on the occasion of the marriage of the Kürfurst Johann George II. of Wittenberg.

For this representation a kind of amphitheatre was constructed. At one end of this was a high wooden platform decorated with cloths and trees. Immediately before it stood a chair for the Tsar. At the base of the amphitheatre was built a special gallery pierced with windows, guarded by lattice work, to accommodate the Tsaritsa and her children.

The performance began with the recitation of complimentary verses addressed to the Tsar, after which there was a *pas de trois* executed by Orpheus and two pirates. Then Orpheus reappeared, splendidly attired, and performed some foreign dances. The entertainment was a great success and pleased the Tsar.

It is of interest to mention the remuneration received by Gregory and the members of his company. The Russian performers received 4 *denga* (equals 2 kopecks) *per diem*, while Gregory received forty sables, each valued at 100 roubles.

Matveyev was commanded to select a certain number of promising children from the burgher classes, and send them to Germany to be trained as actors. A school for the

---

[1] Some authorities give the date as 1675.

theatre was founded, and from time to time performances were given in the Hall of Comedy built in the *Kreml*. Gregory, who had worked so assiduously to create in Russia an interest in the theatre, died in 1675. Deprived of his enthusiasm and encouragement, interest declined, and, on the sudden death of the Tsar in 1676, the performances ceased altogether.

Tsar Alexis was twice married, and Theodore, the eldest surviving son by his first marriage, became heir to the throne at the age of fourteen. During his minority the reactionary party gained power, and the enlightened Matveyev and his group were banished on a charge of sorcery. Theodore's reign was short and uneventful for, always weak in health, he died in 1682, without issue.

PART II

UNDER PETER THE GREAT

(1682–1725)

THEODORE'S brother, Ivan V., a mentally deficient youth of fifteen, and his half-brother, Peter I., then ten years old, were proclaimed joint Tsars under the regency of the Tsarevna Sophia, one of the Tsar Alexis's daughters by his first wife. This lady was active, ambitious, endowed with a strong character, and possessed of a genius for political intrigue. Seven years later she tried to gain complete control of the Government, but Peter, by calling to his aid the young nobles attached to his person and the chiefs of the *Streletsy*[1] who had remained faithful to him, deprived her of power and compelled her to retire into a monastery.

Peter now reigned alone, but still had little authority. The reactionary party again came to the front, and the lonely Tsar cultivated the acquaintance of foreigners, and began to study with a view to self-improvement. His half-brother, Ivan, died in 1696, so that, feeling firm-seated on his throne, in March, 1697, he undertook his first foreign tour, from which he was recalled some eighteen months later by the revolt of the *Streletsy*.

The rebellion was crushed and Peter took a terrible revenge on the persons implicated. Having gained this decisive success, Peter began to work for the development

[1] Lit. Archers, the standing army.

of his people. Reform followed reform, hundreds of foreign experts were imported into Moscovy and hundreds of young Russians were sent abroad to be educated in the European manner. During his travels abroad Peter had been much interested in the ballets and masquerades which he had witnessed. When at Amsterdam in 1697 he had been present at the beautifully-staged ballet *Cupidon*, and in 1698 he had taken part in a masquerade at Vienna, where, disguised as a Friesland peasant, he had danced a great deal.

In 1700, Peter introduced Assemblies, as a result of which the doors of the *terems* were opened, and women permitted to appear in public for the first time. To these Assemblies the Tsar commanded to come men and women of the better classes, all distinguished foreigners and their wives and children—and all were to be dressed in the foreign manner. The consternation caused by this proclamation can well be imagined. Everyone made excuses and the evasions were endless. Unfortunately for the progress of the Dance, Peter commenced war against Sweden, and for the time being had little leisure to devote to the encouragement of the new art.

In 1703, the first public theatre in Russia was constructed near the *Kreml* in Moscow. There were four classes of seats, priced respectively at ten, six, five and three kopecks. There were two performances a week; which generally lasted from 5 to 10 p.m. This theatre, built of wood, was demolished in 1707.

In 1710, when the victory of Poltava (where, in June, 1709,[1] Peter defeated the Swedish invaders under Charles XII.) was celebrated at Moscow, there is a record of an entertainment being given entitled *An Officer's Dance, with Recitative in Praise of Arms and Warriors*.

In 1718, Peter issued very strict orders that for the future Russian women were to take the same status as those abroad. He organised many Assemblies at which he himself danced and forced others to do likewise. Bergholz says: " He made such *caprioles* that any dancing master

---

[1] It was at this period that the Court Theatre was transferred to St. Petersburg, the new capital, the foundations of which had been laid by Peter in 1703.

A BALL FOR DWARVES DURING THE REIGN OF PETER THE GREAT
From Brückner's "Istoriya Petra Velikago"

might envy him." This Tsar is credited with the introduction into Russia of the *Courante*, *Menuet* and *Pavane*.

After the Peace of Nystad in 1721 there was held a great Masquerade which lasted five days. It included a wonderful procession of sixty sledges, the smallest of which was drawn by six horses. At first everyone danced awkwardly at these Assemblies and Masquerades, but Peter and his wife, Catherine, astonished all by their skill and grace. It was on the occasion of this festival that Peter received from the assembled synod and senate the three titles of "Emperor," "Great," and "Father of the Country."

According to one historian, the captured Swedish officers were the first dancing-masters to the Russian ladies and gentlemen. Those who distinguished themselves at the later Assemblies were Count Yaguzhinsky, the Austrian Ambassador, Count Kinsky, the Holstein Minister, M. Bassevich, and the young Princes Trubetskoy and Dolgoruky. Among the ladies were the Grand Duchess Elizabeth Petrovna (daughter of Peter I.), the Princesses Cherkasskaya, Kantemir, Trubetskaya, Dolgorukaya and the Countess Golovkina. The orchestra included hautbois, bassoons, trumpets and kettle drums. At these Assemblies it was customary for the host to present a bouquet to the lady he most admired, and she became the Queen of the Ball. Then, in her turn, she presented her bouquet to a chosen gentleman and intimated to him the day on which she desired to dance at his house. This custom helped to maintain the Assemblies in the public gaze and assist their continuance.

Catherine's Assemblies were generally held after dinner in the gardens of the Summer Palace, the music being supplied by the Preobrazhensky and Semenovsky regiments, and were not inferior in elegance to the best of the petty German courts.

Peter's Assemblies were marked by the manners of the camp. The Tsar and his friends smoked heavily and drank "hollands," and this, combined with the noise of the shuffling of cards and the rattling of dice, chessmen and draughtsmen, made the proceedings more suggestive of a tavern. Dancing continued to midnight in an open gallery overlooking the Neva, and concluded with a magnificent display of fireworks.

More important still were the ordinary public Assemblies at the mansions of the nobles, designed to educate the Russian public in European manners. The rules respecting them may be paraphrased thus—

1. Any person desirous of organising an Assembly at his residence shall cause his intention to be made known by placing outside his dwelling an announcement of the same.

2. No Assembly shall commence before four o'clock in the afternoon, and no Assembly shall conclude later than ten o'clock in the evening.

3. The host of such an Assembly shall neither receive nor assist at the departure of the guests, nor shall he pay them any particular attention. The host, however, shall provide seats for the comfort of the guests, also refreshments, and some form of illumination for the room appointed.

4. Each guest may attend the Assembly at such hour as he or she pleases, and is permitted to sit down, walk or play games.

5. Admittance to the Assembly shall be granted to all persons of rank, all noblemen, the most eminent merchants, shipwrights and lesser government officials, together with their wives and children.

6. A special room shall be provided for the guests' attendants, in order that the apartment for the Assembly shall be entirely free for the guests.

7. Any guests guilty of hauteur or affectation shall be punished with the spread-eagle.[1]

During this reign many foreign dramatic companies visited Russia, such as those of Kunst[2], Mann, and others.

[1] The compulsory draining of a huge bumper sufficient to deprive the offender of his senses.

[2] Kunst died in 1703, when his company was taken over by Otto Fürst, another German manager. Some authorities, however, state that Kunst fled the country in 1704, as the result of his perpetrating a hoax that was not appreciated. He announced that he would present "an entirely new and original piece" on April 1st, 1704. The theatre was packed in consequence, the Tsar himself being present. But when the curtain was raised there was merely a large board bearing the words: "To-day is the first of April." According to these writers, Kunst's company was taken over by Fürst in 1705.

Peter died on January 28th, 1725. This monarch, despite his many licentious and cruel qualities, deserves great praise for his splendid reforms. He rescued his country from barbarism, opened up communications with the greater part of Europe, and contended mercilessly against the old iron-bound customs and religious bigotry which had so long prevented the national development; his whole life was devoted to the service of his people.

PART III

FROM THE ACCESSION OF CATHERINE I
TO THE DEATH OF ANNE

(1725–1740)

ON the death of Peter there arose the difficult problem of finding a successor. The Grand Duke Peter, the only son of the Tsarevich Alexis, was regarded everywhere as the rightful heir. The severity of the reforms introduced under Peter's government had aroused discontent, and his wife Catherine was inseparably associated with that system. But Catherine, having surmised that the Emperor's illness was likely to prove fatal, had, with uncommon circumspection, instructed Menshikov, Tolstoy, and other ministers to exert influence in her behalf. By increasing the pay of the army and securing their support, and by the diplomatic measures instituted by the ministers cited, the balance was swung back in favour of the widowed Empress, who was elected to the throne.

Catherine worked hard to eradicate the many abuses which had existed at the Court of Peter the Great. The swarms of deformed and misshapen beings and coarse buffoons were banished; the vice of drinking, common to both sexes, was considerably repressed. On every hand organisations for the moral improvement of the people were founded. In the sphere of the Dance, balls continued to gain the public favour, and soon became the amusement of

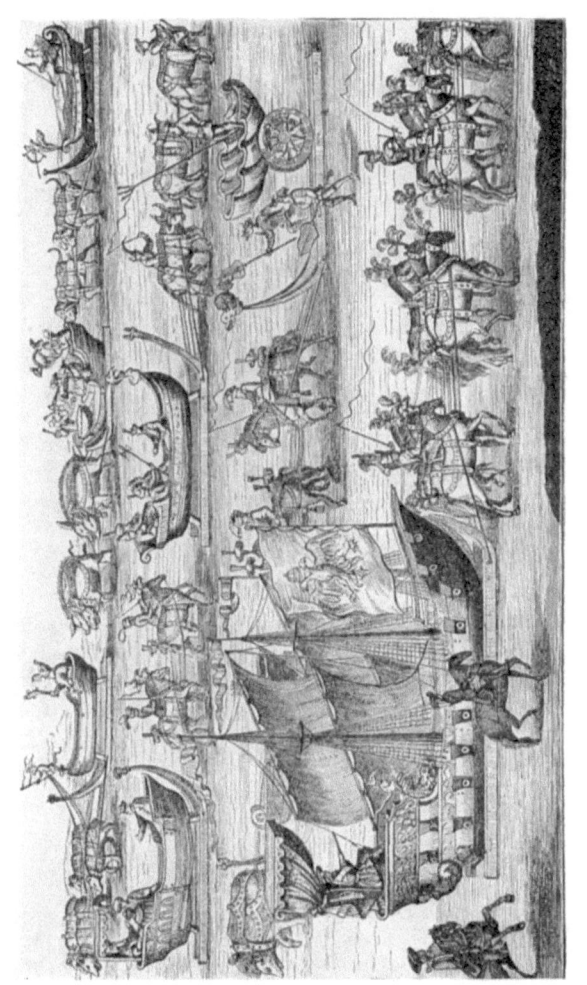

A MASQUERADE DURING THE REIGN OF PETER THE GREAT
From Brückner's "Istoriya Petra Velikago"

every class of society. Dancing became so important a part of the social life that a girl unable to dance was considered to have been brought up badly.

The first ballet performances at St. Petersburg were given in 1727. These spectacles were given at the People's Theatre built by the Green Bridge, now the *Politsei Most* (Police Bridge). The principal dancers were Russian, the volunteer pupils of Otto Fürst. Court ladies and gentlemen danced too, but on the stage of the Winter Palace. The first ballets were *The Fabulous Comedy: With Dances in the German, French, English and Polish Manner;* and *The Bright Falcon's Feather: A Comedy with Songs and Dances.*

Catherine died on May 6th, 1727.

The Grand Duke Peter Alexeyevich, then eleven years old, was proclaimed Emperor. He gave early promise of unusual powers of mind and body, but in 1730 caught small-pox, to which disease he succumbed.

The Princess Anne Ivanovna was elected Empress. At this time she was in her thirty-seventh year. She had married in 1710 (by order of Peter I.) Frederick William, Duke of Kurland. At the wedding feast, Peter caused two immense pies to be placed before the newly married couple, and when he cut the pies open a richly attired dwarf jumped out of each and greatly amused the company by dancing together a *Menuet* on the table.

The Court of Anne was remarkable for its wealth and luxury. Rondeau, the English Resident, wrote in 1731 to Lord Harrington: "Your excellency cannot imagine how magnificent this Court is since the present reign, though there is not a shilling in the treasury, and nobody is paid." A year later he wrote: "I cannot well express how magnificent the Court is in clothes. I never saw such heaps of gold and silver lace laid upon cloth, and even gold and silver stuffs, as are seen here." From these dispatches we learn that to pay £150 to £200 for a suit of clothes was considered nothing unusual at St. Petersburg.

The Empress had inherited from the Tsar Alexis a love of pomp and pageantry. Balls, masquerades and banquets followed each other in endless succession. She had considerable taste for music and dramatic entertainments. The Russian women were more and more encouraged to an easier social intercourse with the other sex, and began to wear dresses planned to set off their charms and ornaments to enhance the effect. The balls were so many, and the *coiffeurs* so few, that the greatest ladies were obliged to have their hair dressed three and four days in advance, and to sleep on chairs for fear of injuring these tonsorial masterpieces.

At the beginning of this reign a fine troupe of actors was sent from Warsaw to Moscow, and so diverted the Empress that for days she could think of nothing else. Augustus II., Elector of Saxony and King of Poland, essayed to gain favour with the Russian Cabinet, by sending an Italian company from Dresden.

On January 1, 1730, there was performed at the People's Theatre, by the Green Bridge, a comedy with music entitled *Orpheus in Hades*, with dances of the spirits devised by O. Fürst. In 1731, a comedy with songs and dances called *Baba Yaga* was given at the Court Theatre; in this danced the Countesses Vorontsova, Apraksina and Bruce, and MM. Shepelev and Strugovshchikov. The principal dancers at the People's Theatre were Mmes. Julia and Volbrik, and M. Ernest. The performances at this theatre ceased on April 25, 1731; the last being *The Destruction of Babylon*. The theatre collapsed on account of its foundations being destroyed by the erosive action of the River Moyka on which it stood.

There are some interesting anecdotes relating to a Court ball given in 1733, in honour of the Ambassadors of Turkey, Bokhara and China. We transcribe them as they are recorded in the correspondence of Lady Rondeau, wife of the English Resident. When the Ball had commenced the Ambassadors were ushered in. The Empress turned to the Chinese Ambassadors and " asked the first of them (for there are three) which he thought the prettiest woman there ? He said, ' It would be difficult in a star-light night to say which star was the brightest '; but observing she expected him to say which he thought so, he bowed to the Princess Elizabeth, ' among such a number of fine women, he thought her the handsomest, and if she had not quite so large eyes, nobody could see her and live.' Her Majesty asked him, of all the things they saw that differed from their own customs, what appeared the most extraordinary? He answered, 'Seeing a woman on the throne.' Soon after this, they were brought to a masquerade at Court and were asked if it did not appear odd to them? They answered, 'No, for all was masquerade to them.'"

As an example of the magnificence displayed at these masquerade balls, we quote this description, written in 1734, also by Lady Rondeau, of that given in the gardens of the Summer Palace, to celebrate the capture of Danzig. "The ladies were dressed in stiffened bodied gowns of white gause (*sic*) with silver flowers; their quilted petticoats, as everyone fancied. . . . On their heads was only their own hair, cut short, and curled in large natural curls and chaplets of flowers. The Empress and the Imperial Family dined in a grotto that faced a long walk terminated by a fountain, and enclosed on each side by an high hedge of Dutch elms. There was a long table the whole length of the walk, which joined at one end to her's in the grotto. Over this long table was a tent of green silk, supported by voluted pillars, which had wreaths of natural flowers twisted round them; between these pillars, in the niches of the hedges, were the sideboards, the whole length of the table, on each side; one furnished with plate, the other with china; the gentlemen drew tickets for their partners, and every man sat by his partner at table; so that a man and woman sat all the way. There were three hundred people at table, and six hundred dishes in a course; two courses and a dessert. . . . After dinner the company separated into parties, and amused themselves in the garden 'till the cool of the evening, when the garden was finely illuminated, and the ball began under the same tent where we dined. The voluted pillars being illuminated had a very pretty effect. The music was placed behind a high hedge, so that it seemed as if the deity of the place supplied that part of the entertainment."

The hall of the Winter Palace used for masquerades was, according to the same informant, considerably larger than St. George's Hall at Windsor. In the coldest weather it was kept quite warm, and decorated with orange trees and myrtles in full bloom, ranged in rows that formed a walk on each side of the hall, only leaving room for the dancers in the centre. The beauty, fragrance and warmth of this artificial grove, when only ice and snow could be seen through the windows outside, had the effect of enchantment.

In 1735, the Empress commanded Christian Friedrich Wellmann, an official at the Infantry School for the Training of Officers' Children, to teach the cadets to dance, so that they could replace the imported Italian dancers. They set to work with great zeal, stimulated by the knowledge that if they succeeded they would appear at Court and have an opportunity of attracting the attention of the Empress. Wellmann was replaced by a Frenchman called Landé, or Landet, who said that " one must go to the Russian Court to see the *Menuet* danced properly." He took girls and boys, the children of poor parents ; Court valets and choir singers ; and organised a school which may be considered as the foundation of the late Imperial Academy of Dancing. He worked hard to prepare solo dancers and a *corps de ballet* for the stage, and received every assistance from Biron, the Empress's all-powerful favourite.

Later in the same year, a good Italian comic dancer, Fuzano, was engaged for ballet in *opera buffa*. In turn, he secured the services of the dancers MM. Tessi and Guiseppe, and the *premières danseuses* Julia Fuzano and Tonina Constantini. His *corps de ballet* was formed from Landé's pupils.

Then the Neapolitan composer Francesco Araja came to Russia to direct the Court Opera Theatre. He made liberal use of Russian melodies in his compositions, and Fuzano reproduced the national dances. From 1736, ballet was frequently given in conjunction with performances of Italian opera.

The Empress ordered two theatres to be built: one for the summer, a Court Theatre, which was constructed near a fir grove ; and one for the winter, to be situated in one of the wings of the Winter Palace.

In 1737, the Empress ordered all young gentlemen to learn arithmetic, writing, reading and dancing.

The excellent beginning made by Fuzano and Araja received a set-back in 1738, when the former incurred Biron's displeasure and was forced to resign and leave Russia. Fuzano revenged himself by inducing his

MASQUERADE GIVEN DURING THE REIGN OF ANNE
From the engraving by Boethius

compatriots to go with him. This troupe went to Paris and London, where they achieved considerable success.

The departure of Fuzano brought Landé into greater prominence. He was engaged at the Court Theatre at an annual salary of 2,000 r. Soon afterwards he was appointed Court *maître de ballet*. The Empress was delighted with the performances given by his pupils, and the Russian Ballet became a recognised institution. It included many capable mimes and dancers: Lebrun, a young Frenchman, who was an excellent dancer, and Timoshka Bublikov, a Little Russian and a member of the Court choir, who had been sent abroad in 1734 to study dancing. The *premiers danseurs* were Afanasy Toporkov and Andrey Nesterov. The *premières danseuses* were Aksinia Sergeyeva, Elizaveta Zorina and Avdotia Timofeyeva, the famous pupil of Julia Fuzano. Landé was highly commended for the result of his labours, received many presents, and was in high favour with Biron and the Court. His school was enlarged and the pupils trained at the expense of the government. In addition, Landé received a special salary as professor. The ballet had now a definite form and proved the existence of national talent; the progress of dancing was no longer entirely dependent on the abilities of foreign artistes.

The school was situated in the *Zimny Dom* (Winter House), for which purpose two rooms on the top floor were set aside. Landé took up his abode in the same building. Theodosia Kurtasova, the widow of a Court stable-boy, was appointed to supervise the female students. Captain Stepan Ramburch was ordered to act as comptroller, and received a specific sum of money and quantity of food for their keep. He was supplied each day with 10 lbs. of best white flour, 1 lb. of second-quality flour, 2 lbs. of butter, 1 *vedro* (20 bottles) of half-beer and 2 *vedra* of *kislyia shchi* (a kind of *kvass*). In regard to illumination, he received daily 5 lbs. of tallow candles in winter and 2 lbs. of candles in summer. He was also allowed a sum of 560 r. for expenditure in connection with the supply of clothing and articles of attire.

The history of the extraordinary development of dancing and ballet in the reign of the Empress Anne can be closed fittingly by a description of the festivities held at St. Petersburg on the occasion of the marriage of the Princess Anne with Prince Antony of Brunswick-Wolfenbuttle, for which we are indebted again to the correspondence of Lady Rondeau. The 30 July, 1739, she writes to her friend in England: "On Friday there was a masquerade; there were four quadrilles, as they are called, consisting of twelve ladies each, besides the leader of each quadrille. The first was led by the bride and bridegroom, who were dressed in orange coloured dominos, and little caps of the same with a silver cockade, and a little laced ruff round the neck, tied with the same ribbon; and their twelve couples were all dressed the same, among whom all the foreign ministers and their wives were placed, whose masters were related either to the Prince or Princess. The second was led by the Princess Elizabeth and Prince Peter, in green dominos and gold cockades, and their twelve couples the same. The third by the Duchess of Courland and Count Soltikoff (a relation of the Empress), in blue dominos and pink and silver cockades. The fourth by her daughter and youngest son, in pink dominos and green and silver cockades. There was a supper for the four quadrilles only, in the long gallery; the table had benches round it, so placed as to look like a turf bank, and the table the same; the table and benches were covered with moss and flowers, stuck in as if growing, and the supper, though very magnificent, was served to look like a rural entertainment. On Sunday there was a masquerade in the garden of the Summer Palace, which was finely illuminated, and a firework in the river which runs by the side of the garden. Everybody dressed to their own fancy, some very pretty, and some very rich ones."

The Empress Anne, who had been ailing for some time, died on October 17th, 1740.

PART IV

FROM THE REGENCY OF BIRON TO THE DEATH OF ELIZABETH

(1740-1796)

THE Empress Anne, by her first will, had appointed her niece, the Duchess of Mecklenburg, as her successor. But during her last days Biron and his friends had persuaded her to sign a new will in favour of her niece's son, Ivan (VI.), whose youth would necessitate a representative governor. Biron then contrived that he should be prayed to accept the Regency. Glorying in his new power, he controlled affairs with a despotic tyranny which soon became insupportable. Jealousy burned fiercely in the breasts of the many important generals and statesmen who, expecting a share in the pickings for their assistance, received only peremptory orders. A new conspiracy was evolved as a result of which Biron was seized and confined in the fortress of Schlüsselburg, from whence he was removed later to the wilds of Siberia.

About this time Landé was sent abroad to engage some foreign dancers. He found an excellent troupe at Cassel and wished to engage them, but they set so high a value on their services that the negotiations lasted a whole year.

In 1741, the Duchess of Brunswick became Regent, and her husband was given the command of the troops, but she committed so many diplomatic blunders that a fresh revolution was prepared. A French surgeon, Lestocq, with the help of the French Ambassador, the Marquis de la Chetardie, induced the Princess Elizabeth Petrovna to make a bid for the throne. At first, terrified of the result of failure, she hesitated; then, in response to continual urgings and reproaches, she assented. The Preobrazhensky Guards, previously seduced by the gold lavishly scattered by the French Ambassador, declared in her favour. The Regent, her husband and son, were imprisoned in the fortress of Schlüsselburg, and her principal ministers banished. It may be enquired for what reason the French Ambassador interested himself in this plot. It was to facilitate an alliance with France and to destroy the rising influence of the Austrian Empress, Maria Theresa.

The reign of Elizabeth had commenced. She was a lady of striking beauty, endowed with a passionate love of pleasure, and renowned for her dancing. According to Shtellin[1], she was "the best dancer of her time who gave an example to her Court of correct and graceful dancing." She also performed the Russian national dances. Foreign artistes visited St. Petersburg in great numbers. Immense sums of money were squandered on Russian artistes, and balls, masquerades and Italian *opera buffa* were in high favour.

When Fuzano, then in Paris, heard that the Princess Elizabeth, whom he knew well, through having contributed to her dancing education, had been proclaimed Empress, he returned post-haste to St. Petersburg, arriving in 1742, to offer his services. He was appointed second Court *maître de ballet* for comic ballets, Landé being retained in his position as *maître de ballet* for dramatic ballets, for the Empress was a sincere admirer of his talent and industry.

On the occasion of the Coronation festivals at Moscow, a theatre was built on the Yausa, a tributary of the River Moskva. And here were presented an opera, *The Mercy of Titus*, a prologue by Schtellin called *La Russia Afflitta e Riconsollatta*, and an allegorical ballet entitled *The Rejoicing of the People because Astrea has appeared on the Russian Horizon and the Golden Age has been established anew*. In the opera

[1] Shtellin and Essipov. *Drevnaya i Novaya Rossiya.*

danced the children taught by Landé. At this time the company numbered thirty. The ballet cited and another called *The Golden Apple at the Feasts of the Gods and the Judgment of Paris*, were produced by Fuzano owing to Landé's absence.

Now and again Lebrun was commanded to produce allegorical ballets, which were invariably successful. The choregraphic firmament was brightened by two new stars: Fuzano's wife Julia, celebrated throughout Europe, and Aksinia Sergeyeva, an exceptionally talented dancer, whose style showed an evident admiration of the art of Julia Fuzano.

The theatre in which opera-ballets were given was a reconstructed riding-school, situated near the Kazan Cathedral. This was a public theatre " open to all decently clad persons." The various classes of seats were allotted according to the spectator's rank. There was no charge for admission, but it was not easy for members of the *bourgeoisie* to obtain a place.

In 1745, on the occasion of the marriage of the Grand Duke Peter Fedorovich (afterwards Peter III.) with the Princess Catherine Alexeyevna[1] (afterwards the Empress Catherine II.), the opera-ballet *Scipio* was performed. The choregraphy was by Fuzano, the music by Araja, the decorations by Valeriani and Bonnat. A short ballet was given between each act of the opera. The principal rôles were distributed thus: Julia Fuzano (*Psyche*), A. Sergeyeva (*Venus*) and T. Lebrun (*Cupid*).

Landé died on February 26th, 1746.

In 1753, Fuzano engaged some new foreign artistes, the dancers Mlles. Colomba and Fabiani, and MM. Fabiani and Tordo.

At this point it is of interest to cite some of the salaries paid to the principal dancers. Julia Fuzano received an annual amount of 1,200 r., her understudy Sergeyeva 350 r., Colomba 1,350 r., Fabiani 1,000 r. The husband of the first-named received 1,000 r., the *premiers danseurs* Gaetano Tordo 1,350 r., Thomas Lebrun 400 r., and

---

[1] Her real name was Sophia and she was the daughter of the Prince of Anhalt-Zerbst. She renounced her membership of the Lutheran to join the Greek Church, in order that she might marry the Grand Duke Peter.

Toporkov 350 r. The conductor Araja was paid 2,000 r., the architect and scene-painter Valeriani 2,000 r.

The *danseuse* Sergeyeva died on January 27th, 1756.

In 1757, the well-known impresario Giovanni Locatelli visited St. Petersburg with a company of *opera buffa* singers and a troupe of ballet dancers. Through the good-will of the Empress, Locatelli was enabled to secure the possession of an old Opera House near the *Letny Sad* (Summer Garden). Here members of the aristocracy and wealthy townsfolk could rent a box, which they could decorate according to their taste, for an annual subscription of 300 r. The poorer classes paid an admittance fee of 1 r. per performance. The Empress often visited the theatre incognito, and was sufficiently pleased by the entertainments afforded to grant Locatelli an annual subsidy of 5,000 r.

At this period there was a considerable display of hero-worship. Each *danseuse* had her own particular group of admirers. There were no partisan outbursts of clapping and shouting; the spectators proclaimed their fancies by wearing small cards inscribed with the names of their favourite dancers. The principal artistes of Locatelli's troupe were M. and Mme. Saccho, Mmes. Andriani and Beluzi, and MM. Caesar, Olivier and Kolzevaro.

Here is a list of the ballets performed: *Orpheus and Eurydice*, *A Post House at London*, *Apollo and Daphnis*, *The Rape of Proserpine*, and *Cleopatra's Feast*. The first three were by Locatelli and Saccho, the last two by Saccho. Several Russian dancers took part in these spectacles, including Mmes. Afanasieva, Varvara, Mikhaylova, Timofeyeva and Fedorova, and MM. Afanasiev, Krilov and Vasiliev. According to a contemporary, Locatelli's productions were distinguished as much by their taste as by their originality, and " it was impossible to see a better company in the whole of Europe."

Locatelli's successor in ballet productions was Hilferding, who arrived at St. Petersburg in 1759. He was a very talented *maître de ballet*, and formerly had been attached to the Austrian Court, which, desirous of pleasing Elizabeth, had sent him to Russia. His ballets were much liked, especially *The Victory of Flora over Boreas*, performed at the Winter Palace on February 26th, 1761. The music was by

Starzer, and the decorations by Brigonzo. The cast was: Hilferding (*Jupiter*), M. Mercure (*Boreas*), Mme. Santini-Ubri (*Flora*), Mme. Mercure (*Diana*), M. Prior (*Zephyr*), M. Paradise (*Mercury*), Mme. Prior (*Minerva*) and M. Taulato (*Pluto*). Starzer was an excellent composer of ballet music and a good conductor. According to Shtellin,[1] the Russian dancers became greatly improved in their work as a result of Hilferding's talent and assiduity. His troupe was the first to perform in Russia the *entrechat-quatre* and the *pirouette*. He also introduced pastoral ballets with themes descriptive of the loves of shepherds and shepherdesses.

At Oranienbaum, where the Grand Duke Peter and his wife resided, there were given some ballet performances by Kolzevaro. His conductor was Starzer, and he had the same troupe as Hilferding. The performances at Oranienbaum were given in the summer only. In 1761, Kolzevaro became ill, and left Russia to go abroad. Among his ballets were *The Golden Branch*, *The Chinese Imperial Marriage* and *A Peasant Festival at St. Petersburg during Carnival*. On December 23rd, 1761, a ballet by Lebrun, entitled *Dido and Æneas*, was given at the *Letny Sad*.

Two days later the Empress Elizabeth died.

[1] *Op. cit.*

PART V

FROM THE ACCESSION OF PETER III. TO THE DEATH OF CATHERINE II.

(1762–1796)

IN 1744, the Empress Elizabeth had already appointed as her successor Peter, son of the Duke of Holstein-Gottorp and Anne, daughter of Peter I. The new Emperor immediately concluded peace with Prussia, then suppressed secret torture, and freed the slaves on the immense lands owned by the clergy and annexed their domains to the crown. He improved the legal tribunals and devoted himself to the study of commerce, the arts and the sciences. Unfortunately his endeavours were militated against by his mania for the introduction of German manners into both court and camp. Frederick the Great, who had been soundly thrashed by the Austro-Russian army in the previous reign, received back at his hands more fortresses, towns and prisoners than he would have dared to ask had he been victorious.

Peter III. was on ill terms with his wife, so much so that he meditated punishing her indiscretions with the axe. Catherine, only too conscious of his thoughts, prepared to act quickly lest the blow should fall. A conspiracy was formed, headed by her lover Gregory Orlov, the Hetman Razumovsky and Count Panin, to seize the throne on her behalf. The troops at St. Petersburg were won over with the usual heavy bribery and, when Peter had departed to

Peterhov, Catherine was proclaimed Empress. On June 29th, Peter went to Oranienbaum. He was arrested the next day and imprisoned in the castle of Ropscha.

On July 6th, Alexis, a brother of Gregory Orlov, accompanied by an assassin, went to visit the deposed monarch. He accepted their offer to drink with them, but instead of the promised brandy they contrived to fill his cup with poison. The unfortunate Emperor, however, suspicious of the flavour of the beverage, refused to continue drinking, and began to scream for milk. Disregarding his cries, the two murderers sprang upon their victim and strangled him to death.

Owing to the mourning for the Empress Elizabeth, no performances were given during the brief reign of Peter III., with the exception of a drama called *The Heroes' Peace*, performed at the *Letny Sad* on the occasion of the peace with Prussia.

During the reign of Catherine II. public taste developed rapidly, and never before in Russia were people so interested in the theatre. Many nobles and wealthy merchants ruined themselves in their endeavours to rival each other in the prevailing fashion. The Empress herself wrote plays and superintended performances; every production, musical and choregraphic, was an event of importance. A ballet was given after each act of an opera, when dancers expressed in mime the meaning of the words sung by the singers. Good ballet was preferred to indifferent opera.

The teaching of pupils was continued with great zeal. One of the best known professors of dancing was Poché. His title was *Director of Social Entertainments at the Infantry Cadet School of St. Petersburg*. He produced many "faeries," with ballets, for which purpose a large amphitheatre was constructed in the school garden. In 1775, he organised a beautiful performance on the occasion of the signing of peace with Turkey.

The choregraphic art developed considerably owing to the many new ballets produced and the number of old ones revived, and on account of the many celebrated dancers and *maîtres de ballet* associated in their representation.

On December 20th, 1762, Locatelli was accorded permission to organise five masquerades during the season at

St. Petersburg, subject to certain regulations, the principal being that no guest could carry arms. These entertainments were very popular, and for several years Locatelli was invited to arrange new ones. They were often used for official entertainments, and the State contributed a sum to defray part of his expenses.

Masquerades were also held at Moscow. In order to show how they were appreciated it is interesting to give an idea of Locatelli's receipts. At a masquerade given in Moscow on February 19th, 1766, there must have been many guests, since the Court alone purchased 1,808 tickets, each priced at 2 r. On April 22nd, in the same year, the Court purchased, for another masquerade, tickets to the value of 4,792 r. The direction of the theatre, seeing that Locatelli was thriving exceedingly, sold the right to give masquerades to a M. Felcht. But at the beginning of the nineteenth century, when his contract had expired, they retained the monopoly and made, for several years at St. Petersburg, an annual net profit of from 60,000 r. to 70,000 r., with an entrance fee of 1 r. only. Locatelli became the proprietor of the New Opera House at Moscow, but he suffered severe financial loss as a result of his new venture, and finally ended as professor of Italian at the Theatre School.

Ballet performances started in Moscow on the occasion of the Coronation of Catherine II., and were continued until June, 1763, when the Court returned to St. Petersburg. The Moscow performances were given in the Court Theatre, at the *Kreml*, and at the theatre opposite the Golovinsky Palace. There was an interesting ballet given at the Court Theatre, entitled *The Joyful Return of the Goddess of Spring to the Arcadian Shepherds and Shepherdesses*. It was performed entirely by the ladies and gentlemen of the Court.

On January 30th and February 1st and 2nd, 1763, during Carnival, Moscow witnessed a great processional masquerade called *Minerva Triumphant*. This was a fine spectacle, not only on account of the splendid costumes and *tableaux*, but for the interesting theme devised by the dramatic artiste, T. Volkov. The rhymed libretto was by Sumarakov, the choruses by * * * (Kheraskov). Over

4,000 people and 200 chariots took part in the procession. Here is an extract from the announcement of it :—

> This month, from ten o'clock in the morning until the afternoon, there will be a grand masquerade procession entitled *Minerva Triumphant*, in which the Abomination of Vice and the Glory of Virtue will be shown. After the return of the procession to the Ice Mountain, the members of it will toboggan and perform different dances, puppet comedies, tricks and so on, at a specially constructed theatre. The artistes will be awarded prizes for their talent. There will be riding also. People of every denomination may attend there if they wish, and toboggan the whole week from morning to night, with or without a mask, as may be thought convenient.[1]

After the Court had returned to St. Petersburg, a ballet was given at Peterhov on the anniversary of the Empress's accession to the throne. This was a revival of *The Joyful Return of the Goddess of Spring to the Arcadian Shepherds and Shepherdesses*. V. O. Mikhnevich[1] states that after the expiration of the period of mourning for Peter III., the Court Theatre was opened by an opera entitled *Olympiade*, which included a ballet composed by Hilferding, who soon afterwards left Russia. He was accompanied by the composer Starzer and the *danseuse* Santini-Ubri, who returned the following year.

She was replaced during her absence by the *demi-caractère danseuse* Fusi, who made her *début* in 1764 in the opera-ballet *Charles the Great*. Santini-Ubri, on her return, remained in the ballet until 1783. About the time that Hilferding left Russia, Bublikov returned. It will be remembered that he had been sent abroad to perfect his talent.

When *Atys and Galatea* was given in 1765, Paul Petrovich, the son of Peter III. and Catherine II., expressed a desire to dance in it, and the fact that he took part in the rehearsals shows the high esteem in which ballet was held. Many courtiers and officers of the Imperial Guard danced in this production. Among those who distinguished themselves were A. P. Sheremeteva, the maid of honour Khitrovo and the Princess Khovanskaya. The Grand Duke astonished every one by his noble bearing and graceful manners. He was taught by the *maîtres de ballet* Grandjé and Hilferding. During this epoch the success of the ballet performances

[1] Quoted Pleshchayev, *Nash Balet*, p. 46.

was due to Grandjé, and the *maîtres de ballet* and dancers Angiolini, Le Picq and Canziani.

It is important to give some details of these four celebrities. The ballets of Pierre Grandjé were much admired, especially *The Shipwreck and Deliverance from Ethiopian Captivity*, *Atys and Galatea*, *Apollo and Daphnis*, and the opera-ballet *Armida*. In the first danced Grandjé himself, Mme. Fusi and MM. Caesar and Paradise; the last named was considered a very talented dancer and produced some successful ballets of his own.

Angiolini received a yearly salary of 4,500 r., an apartment, and 30 *sajen* of wood. He made his *début* in an heroic ballet, composed by himself, entitled *Dido Abandoned*. In 1768 he produced at Moscow a national Russian ballet, for which he also composed the music. In *Dido Abandoned* the principal *danseuse* was Mme. Santini-Ubri; the part of Jarb was played by Angiolini, and that of Jarb's favourite by Bublikov. When Angiolini left the stage he was awarded a considerable pension.

Charles Le Picq was considered to be a *maître de ballet* of the first order and, as a dancer,[1] equal to Vestris and Dauberval in France. He directed the dances for, and took part in, the marvellous spectacle given at the Taurida Palace by Prince Potemkim,[2] the Empress's favourite, in 1791, the production of which entailed an expenditure of over

[1] Grimm describes him thus: " Charming features, the most slender body, the easiest and lightest movements, the purest, most spirited and most natural precision, such are the qualities which distinguish Lepic. If he does not dance like God the Father, at least he dances like the King of Sylphs. He has elasticity and brilliance. His grace and airiness triumph above all in *demi-caractère* dancing." (See Grimm et Diderot, *Correspondance Littéraire, Philosophique et Critique adressée à un Souverain d'Allemagne*, 1812–14.)

[2] This prince took count of neither time, space nor money in ministering to his insatiable passion for pleasure. On one occasion in 1791, when at Bender, in the course of the Second Turkish War, he became seized with the desire to see a *tzigane* danced. He causes inquiries to be made and learns that two young men, formerly sergeants in the Guards, were famous for their execution of this dance. But it is found that they have been promoted and since risen to captains in a regiment stationed in the Caucasus, nearly a thousand miles distant. A messenger is at once dispatched and the officers are recalled. When they have arrived, they dress as a peasant man and woman and for a week dance each night before the favourite. When he had tired of this amusement, he promoted the officers to be majors and ordered them back to their regiments.

500,000 r. The musicians were concealed in enormous chandeliers and the Grand Dukes Alexander and Constantine at the head of a company of young nobles, all attired in white velvet, danced a ballet, after which they sang an ode in praise of the Empress. Le Picq received an annual salary of 6,000 r., and the right to occupy, when he wished, a special box on the third floor of the theatre. The other dancers had only one box between them. He composed many ballets, such as *The Beautiful Arsena, Cupid and Psyche, The Death of Hercules*, etc. He appeared in the ballets *The Oracle, Tancred, The Two Savoyards* and others. In the last-named danced Mme. G. Le Picq (Rossi), at that time principal dancer. She achieved great success in the ballets *Alexander Compast* and *Adèle de Ponthieu*.

Joseph Canziani succeeded Angiolini in 1787. Prior to this post he taught dancing to the young pupils at the Theatre School. He attained a salary of 5,500 r., and retired with a pension in 1792. His best ballets were *Ariadne and Bacchus, The False Deaf Mute, Vanquished Prejudices* and *Pyramus and Thisbe*.

During the reign of Catherine, several performances were given at the *Smolny Monastyr*, a school for young ladies of the nobility. The Empress was present on such occasions. Many articles concerning these performances were published in the *S. Peterburgsky Vyedomosty*, from one of which the following quotation is taken, regarding that given on July 19th, 1775:

Description of a Pleasant Performance which took place on July 19, 1775, at the School for the Young Ladies of the Nobility in the presence of pupils invited from the first five classes.

These persons were received in the Great Hall by four girls of the white class dressed as Vestals. The walls were decorated from top to bottom with greenery, and pyramids and garlands of flowers surmounted with inscriptions in Russian, German, Italian and French. At the summit of the hall were figures symbolical of Benevolence and Charity. At the bottom of the hall were avenues of orange trees decorated with garlands of flowers. On the floor, at one end, was erected the Hill of Parnassus.

From this hall the assembled people went to a garden, at the entrance of which were built two large amphitheatres, occupied by the girls who took no part in the performance. A wattle-hedge of green plants, connected by garlands to the orange trees, decorated the main avenue. There were six niches, decorated with flowers and greenery, in which small stages were erected; on these the girls gave different performances. One was very harmonious, the others were like introductions to the Grand Performance called *La Rosière de Salency* which was given in the large theatre at the end of the main passage.

When the guests arrived they saw the Temple of Benevolence, its entrance hidden by a mountain; and shepherdesses went down the mountain to present gifts to the Rosière. They expressed their joy by pastoral dances. When Benevolence crowned the shepherds with flowers to the sounds of music, the mountain opened and revealed the inside of the temple, where stood an altar on which a sacred flame was burning. It was surrounded by an amphitheatre with seventy Vestals in it who attended to the fire. Forty shepherdesses and forty peasant girls, who were seen on the lowest steps, danced. Three Graces and the Vestals joined them. These concluded the play with a dance in which they held garlands of flowers above their heads and moved them so that they resembled a living garden.

Then the doors in the main passage were thrown open and the guests could see on each side the tables laid for supper, of which all the girls, save the Vestals, partook. Afterwards, the guests, on returning to the main hall, saw on the Hill of Parnassus the Vestals, four of whom (of the burgher class) received them and played music on two flutes, a violin and cello. After that a concert on two harps was given and then a choir sang in Russian a song of greeting and expressed the general joy which filled them. Then the Vestals sat at the tables and took their supper.[1]

The professors of dancing at the Theatre School were Canziani, Valberg and Gugliemi.

At the end of the 'seventies the pupils of the Foundling School took part in performances. They were brought from Moscow and given to the impresario Knipper, who taught them theatrical art, music and dances. But afterwards this practice was discontinued.

The ballets produced during the second half of the reign of Catherine II. were given at the Wooden Theatre at the *Tsaritsin Loug* (Tsaritsa's Lawn), and in the Stone or *Bolshoy* (Great) Theatre situated between the little river Moyka and the Ekaterininsky Canal and, less frequently, at the Hermitage and Tsarskoe Selo Theatres. *Dido Abandoned* was performed at the Bolshoy Theatre. During the performance a firework was let off and a dummy elephant, with a boy on its back, appeared on the stage.

Other ballets given were *Adonis Transformed into a Flower; Alexander Compast; l'Amour Vengé; Cupid and Psyche, Annette and Lubim; Ariadne and Bacchus; Harlequin, Patron of Fairies; Atys and Galatea; La Bergère* (Le Picq); *Boreas; A Magnanimous Pardon; The Traitor, or A Woman Hero; The Caliph of Cordova; Cortonato; Lauretta* (Gugliemi); *Medea and Jason; Mekeleti; The Miller* (Auguste); *The*

---

[1] Quoted Pleshchayev, *op. cit.*, p. 48.

Conquered Pirates; The False Deaf Mute; A Happy Repentance; The Three Hunchbacks; The Gypsies, and others.

During this reign the painting of theatrical scenery made great progress. Three of the most prominent artists were Joseph Valeriani, Franz Graditious and Pietro Gonzago. The first was a painter well known in the 'fifties. Graditious was styled *Her Imperial Majesty's First Artist-Painter, Architect and Engineer.* He served from 1762, and executed many scenes for ballets such as *Flore et Zéphyre, Martodonis, Metamorphoses,* and for many Italian operas. In 1792 he was succeeded by Gonzago, who taught decorative painting to several pupils. He was a celebrity and received an annual salary of 12,500 r. He painted the scenery for *Cupid and Psyche, Tancred* and others. His best pupil was Alexeyev.

The most prominent dancers during the reign of Catherine II. were MM. Hilferding, Angiolini, Grandjé, Le Picq, Canziani, Antonio Cianfanelli, Rosetti, Gugliemi, Jean Schwabe, Casassi, Rossi, Caesar, I. Valberg, P. Columbus, Balashov, J. Stakelberg, Scalesi, Pinucci, Stellato, T. Slebkin, Paradise, Yeropkin, Sychev, Taulato, Pitro, Fabiani, Bublikov and Gladyshev; and Mlles. Le Picq (Rossi), Caterina Coppini (Cianfanelli), Stellato, Theresa Schwabe, Piemontesi, Mercure-Prati, Grandjé, Santini-Ubri, Fusi, Mercure, Maria Grekova, Timofeyeva and Alexandrova.

An important dancer in this reign was Liesogorov, whom the Empress called Valberg. He was the first Russian *maître de ballet,* and so occupies an important place in history.

The most talented of the younger *danseuses* were Nastasia Parfentievna Birilova, known as Nastenka, and O. D. Karatyghina, known as Lenushka.

Birilova was born on October 29th, 1778, and became *première danseuse* of the Court Theatre. According to contemporaries she was the incarnation of grace, but died on January 12th, 1804. She received a yearly salary of 1,300 r., 150 r. annually for apartments, 20 *sajen* of wood for heating and 10 r. monthly for shoes and stockings. She danced in the ballet *The Oracle,* but only at the end of the century. According to legend she was buried in a grave lined with furs, and covered with flowers instead of earth.

Karatyghina was the daughter of D. V. Karatyghin, the Comptroller of the Household of the Theatre School. She made her first appearance at the Hermitage Theatre in 1789.

Spectacles were organised everywhere and the interest in the arts was widespread. The arts flourished on account of the Empress's sympathy for, and interest in, them. A person who displayed talent was helped, supported and praised. If, at the beginning of this reign, the arts were a luxury, by the end they became a necessity.

Catherine II. died on November 6th, 1796.

PART VI

UNDER PAUL I.

(1796–1801)

CATHERINE was succeeded by her son Paul I., who began his reign with many acts of liberality and clemency, which seemed to augur well for the future; but he had a certain strain of meanness in his character which prevented him from being generous.

He was a passionate admirer of Frederick the Great and the Prussian military system, which he had reproduced with infallible accuracy during his residence at Gatchina, where he was permitted the use of some 2,000 troops of all arms for his experiments. Surrounded from his childhood by spies and filled with the constant fear of being murdered like his father, he had early grown silent and moody. He was a martinet for discipline, severe, capricious and eccentric; in short, his harassed life had warped his character and, not unnaturally, made him suspicious of everyone.

His love of reform brought about his ruin. His first unwise step was to incorporate his little Gatchina army into the Guard, and make all wear "Gatchina kit." The Russian soldier hated the skin-tight Prussian uniform, loathed having to plaster his hair with grease and flour, and bitterly resented having to spend an hour buttoning his black spatter-dashes. Paul further decreed that the

Guard were no longer to be ornamental, but to undergo the same fatigues as the soldiers of the line.

He prohibited the wearing of round hats, for which he had a singular aversion; ordered that horses were to be harnessed in the German fashion. None could use certain colours—green, dark blue, white, red, and strawberry—which were for his service alone. No Russian was allowed to pass beyond the frontiers. All books entering the country were censored. Ukase followed ukase in bewildering succession, and the slightest offence was punished with a beating, degradation, or exile to Siberia.

The most rigid forms of etiquette and ceremony were instituted. If a person were permitted to kiss the Emperor's hand, he had to strike the floor with his knee and give the salute so that it was clearly heard. At the Court Balls the dancers were obliged to twist themselves in every possible way to avoid turning their backs on him. Paul forbade the *Valse* to be danced, regarding it as immodest; but in 1798, when he was enamoured of Mlle. Lapukhina (afterwards Princess Gagarina), he withdrew the ban, at her entreaty.

Though ballets were often performed, the art did not progress. One obstacle to this was the engagement of an incompetent *maître de ballet*, Chevalier, the husband of a French actress, who was the mistress of Count Kutaisov, the Emperor's favourite. This lady was a friend of Barras and in the pay of the First Consul's police during her residence at St. Petersburg.

The husband was occupied solely in making money out of his wife's success. His incapacity as a dancer was only equalled by the insolence of his manners, although he declared that at Paris he had danced with Gardel and Vestris. Owing to his wife's influence he was engaged in 1798 with a salary of 3,300 r., and in four months' time the contract was cancelled and he was granted 4,000 r. On November 9th, 1799, he was appointed by an Imperial decree to be *maître de ballet*. He composed the following ballets: *L'Enlèvement*, *Gaston de Foix*, and *A Village Heroine*.

With Chevalier was engaged the dancer Auguste (Poireau), his wife's brother, who married Le Picq's daughter. A handsome youth, he had danced at the Paris Opéra and was a good mime. He began with a salary of 2,300 r., which was soon afterwards raised to 4,000 r. In 1801, he was granted a benefit. He wrote a ballet, *The Miller*, which was performed in 1784, before his entry in the Russian ballet.

The Emperor detested male dancers, and ordered such parts to be taken by *danseuses*. This was exactly opposed to the views of Elizabeth and Catherine, who, when planning masquerades, always required them to include a number of men dressed as women. Among those who assumed masculine rôles was Nastenka Birilova. She was well built and so adapted for the purpose; but she lacked the necessary strength for supporting work.

The ballets were performed at the Bolshoy, Derevianny (Wooden), and Hermitage Theatres. The prices of the seats at the first-named were increased, but when the theatre was closed for the period of mourning in memory of the Empress, the direction received a subsidy from the Emperor. Later, this was made a State grant; nevertheless, at the death of Paul the management reported a deficit of 292,166 r. This arose from the ballets being produced with great luxury, especially those of Chevalier.

In 1800, the Emperor ordered the director to begin the performances at five in the afternoon and conclude them at eight in the evening. In addition to the artistes and supers, the children employed in the Court Tapestry Manufactory took part in the big ballets; they were dressed as *amorini*.

The celebrated Le Picq continued to be *maître de ballet*, and his ballet *Medea and Jason*, performed in the last years of the eighteenth century, achieved a great success.

In 1800, Ivan Valberg (Liesogorov) was appointed *maître de ballet*, and soon afterwards was sent to Chklov to seek for dancers of talent. He was taught by Canziani and finished his training in 1786. In 1794, he was appointed inspector of the theatre and director of the school of dancing, in which he gave lessons. He took part in the ballets *The Oracle* and *The Deserter*, and composed dances for the French comedy *The Amorous Adventures of a Boyard*, and the ballet *The New Werther*.

Valberg married the dancer Sophia Petrova. He distinguished himself during the reign of Catherine II. and improved his talent by studies abroad. He translated many plays and produced several tragedies and opera-ballets.

The ballet repertory from 1796–1801 was as follows:—
Adèle de Ponthieu.
L'Amour de Flore.
Cupid and Psyche (pantomime ballet by Le Picq).
Armida.
Gaston de Foix (Chevalier).
The Village Heroine (Chevalier).
L'Enlèvement (Chevalier).
An Offering to Cupid (Le Picq).
Love is Happiness (Le Picq).
A Bayard's Love (Le Picq).
The Kindhearted Gentleman } produced by Valberg in
The Nymphs and the Hunter } 1799.
The New Werther.
The Deceived Lovers.
The Oracle (produced in 1797 at the Gatchina Theatre, and a year later at the Pavlovsky Theatre).

In these ballets the following dancers took part: Mlles. Ekaterina Azarevicheva, Nastenka Birilova, Maria Grekova, Rosa Colinette, Evgenia Kolosova, Gertrude Le Picq (Rossi), Wilhelmine Le Picq, Constancia Pleten, Riccardi and Tukmanova, and MM. Balashev, Chevalier, Le Picq, Notta, Auguste (Poireau), and Valberg.

Towards the end of his reign, Paul ordered C. L. Didelot, an eminent *maître de ballet* of the period, to be engaged. With his arrival the choregraphic art steadily rose to a high level.

Mention has been made of the numerous and unwelcome reforms introduced by Paul. Not only were they frequently passed before their effect had been calculated, but they were put into force before anyone had had time to understand them. The Emperor grew more and more suspicious, more and more vindictive were his wishes crossed. Everyone, from a grand duke to the meanest serf, lived in a state of fearful uncertainty. None knew but what the next day would see him on the road to Siberia. Paul tried to curb all abuses and to protect the weak from

THE BOLSHOY THEATRE, ST. PETERSBURG.—EARLY 19TH CENTURY
From a contemporary etching

the strong. But, in interfering with the welfare and pleasures of the higher classes, he encouraged the growth of a conspiracy which finally overwhelmed him.

March 11th, 1801, was the day chosen for the deed. Some sixty conspirators were concerned in the plot, including such distinguished persons as the Zubovs, General Count Benningsen and Count Pahlen. On the fateful night the Emperor retired early to bed, and soon afterwards the conspirators went to his apartment, the outer door of which was opened to them on the demand of an *aide-de-camp* called Argamakhov, who pretended he had to make a report. A Cossack, however, opposed their entrance to the bedroom. He was cut down and the assassins burst in. The Emperor was found, not in bed, but concealed behind a screen. He made a desperate resistance, but a sash was slipped about his neck and he was strangled to death.

PART VII

UNDER ALEXANDER I.

(1801–1825)

ON the death of Paul there was a universal sigh all over Russia, not of regret at his passing, but as though some terrible crisis had passed. The accession of his son Alexander was hailed with joy. He was twenty-five years of age, of majestic figure and noble countenance.

The new Emperor began his reign with many reforms, but all directed at repairing the tyranny of his father's laws and procuring his subjects some sense of liberty and security. He relaxed the rigour of the censorship of the Press, granted permission to introduce foreign works, forbade punishment by torture, prohibited the making of grants of peasants, promoted general education and removed the ban on foreign travel.

Where all was gloom there were smiles and laughter. Six-hand carriages rattled through the streets with a gay jingling of bells. Russians who had been living abroad now returned, bringing with them the latest fashions. The French tongue was all the vogue. It was the birth of a new Golden Age for the Arts.

Alexander was personally very interested in the theatre and settled all questions. Soon after his accession it had been proposed to raise the fees, but the Emperor decided that this was opposed to the public interest and ordered them to remain as before. Wealthy persons of taste devoted themselves to the development of the theatre; already there were connoisseurs of ballet.

During the Coronation some performances took place at the Petrovsky Theatre, Moscow. The season opened on October 2nd with a prologue called *The Temple of Joy*; and a comedy in four acts, by Kotzebue, entitled *The Reconciliation of Two Brothers*. On the 6th, an opera was performed, followed by a comic ballet styled *The Madmen*, by the *maître de ballet* Solomon. On the 20th, another opera, *Cosara*, was produced, and an appropriate ballet called *A Shepherd's Diversion*. On the 22nd, *The Grumbler*, a comedy by Kotzebue, an opera *Theodul and his Children*, and a ballet in which Russian dances were performed. On the 25th, an opera *A Fair at Venice*, and a ballet, *The Power of Love*, by Solomon. On the 30th, another opera, entitled *A Sleeping Powder, or the Kidnapped Peasant*, and a ballet, which pleased owing to the buffoonery of an actor called Raikov. Then all performances ceased until November 4th, which was the end of the appointed period of mourning.

Among the great artistes of this epoch was Didelot, an outstanding personality endowed with extraordinary æsthetic taste. In fact, the ballet underwent so great a transformation under his direction that the history of Russian choregraphy may be divided into two main periods—before Didelot and after Didelot. True, the ballet changed its direction according to the growth of the public taste, but retained its essential character.

Now ballet with miming was in vogue, now dances requiring a high technical ability and perfection of *plastique*. The mythological ballet gave place to the romantic. But these changes did not affect the development of Russian ballet, because its fundamentals became traditional and fixed.

Charles Louis Didelot was born at Stockholm in 1767. His father, a Frenchman, was *premier danseur* at the Stockholm Theatre, and taught dancing to the pupils of the elementary class. He dreamed that his son would be crowned with laurels, for he was short, well-built, strong, intelligent and of lively disposition. But when Charles was six years old he caught small-pox, which marred his features, and the father saw all his hopes ruined.

Fate, however, changed the situation. The brother of the Swedish king, Gustavus III., wished to appear at a Court masquerade as a Savoyard. At the last moment he could not find his marmot, and Didelot was asked to select from his pupils a small and intelligent boy who could take the part. There were, however, no short boys in the class, and, being desperate, the father had his son dressed in a skin with a marmot's head. The youthful debutant made an excellent impression.

Two years later, Charles appeared on the stage of the Stockholm Theatre in the rôle of Cupid. By the King's order he was sent to Paris to study dancing under the celebrated Dauberval. When he had attained some fourteen years old he returned to Stockholm, where he executed some *pas* of his own composition, which pleased greatly. As a consequence he, despite his youth, was charged to arrange the dances for a ballet called *Freya*, which achieved considerable success.

He was again sent to Paris, where he studied under Auguste Vestris. The celebrated Noverre made a contract with Didelot for London, by which he received the sum of £400 for the season. The latter produced there his own ballet *Richard, Cœur de Lion*, and, on account of its favourable reception, his contract was renewed for several years.

Didelot made his first appearance at the Paris Opéra in 1790, with Mlle. Guimard, in Maximilien Gardel's ballet *Le Premier Navigateur*. He then made a short appearance at the Théâtre Montausier, and went to Lyon and London, where he was well received. In 1796 he produced his best ballet, *Flore et Zéphyre*, which earned for him a great reputation. In this ballet Didelot, for the first time, made use of wires for the purpose of enabling dancers to simulate aërial flight, producing effects which astonished the audience. He returned to Paris and again danced with Mlle. Guimard at the Opéra, also at Bordeaux and Lyon.

In 1801, Didelot went to St. Petersburg, where he contributed considerably to the development of the national ballet. He produced *Apollo and Daphnis* in April, 1802;

IVAN VALBERG (LIESOGOROV)

CHARLES DIDELOT

then *Faun and Hamadryad, Cupid and Psyche, Laura and Henry*, and *Roland and Morgana*. His ballets did not require special funds from the direction, but they attracted a large public; partly on account of their beauty, partly on account of the novelty of their stage effects.

Apart from his talents as a dancer and *maître de ballet*, he was a fine teacher. Here is a prose portrait of him. A contemporary, describing a *ballet-divertissement* given in December, 1806, mentions a *pas de deux* performed by Didelot and Ikonina, respectively as Apollo and Diana. He declares that the famous dancer was "as thin as a skeleton, had a very long red nose, wore a light-red wig and a laurel wreath on his head, and danced with a lyre in his hand, with great success. But he evoked a caricature rather than the Sun God."

Another writer, A. Y. Golovacheva-Panaeva, says that Didelot resembled a snipe, and that she could not bear him because he used to beat his pupils. The children returned home from class with bruises on their arms and legs; even his son was not exempt from such treatment.

"It was very amusing to see Didelot behind the scenes watching his pupils. Sometimes he swayed from side to side, smiled, and took mincing steps and stamped his foot. But when the little pupils danced he shook his fist at them, and, if they missed the figures, he made their lives a misery. He pounced on them like a hawk, pulled their hair or ears, and if any ran away he gave them a kick which sent them flying. Even the solo dancers suffered from him. Being applauded, a dancer went behind the scenes, when Didelot seized her by the shoulders, shook her with all his might and, having given her a punch in the back, pushed her on to the stage as if she were recalled."[1]

Outside the theatre Didelot was very kind to his pupils, and helped and kissed those whom he had punched but an hour before. These were the conditions under which the ballet was formed and, however cruel and unjustifiable they may seem, it is of interest to note that the members of the *corps de ballet* were uniformly exceptionally talented. The flying of some of the groups was wonderful; the dancers could soar forward and stop at the very edge of the footlights.

[1] Quoted Pleshchayev, *op. cit.*, p. 59.

However, notwithstanding his fame and excellent position in Russia, Didelot longed to be acclaimed in Paris as a *maître de ballet*. Accordingly, in 1811, he set out for that capital, but on his journey from St. Petersburg to Lübeck he suffered shipwreck, lost all his music, all his choregraphic notes and narrowly escaped with his life. This was only the beginning of a series of misfortunes which followed in quick succession.

He was anxious to produce his *Flore et Zéphyre*, but Gardel, who was in high favour at the Opéra, was jealous of the ballet's renown and, as a result of his intrigues, months, even years, passed before Didelot achieved his aim. The management having raised all manner of polite objections, informed him that his ballet would be too expensive to mount, and that they could not produce it unless he would guarantee to pay all the expenses in advance.

Didelot was much offended, but agreed. Now it was necessary to have a special scene made to conceal the wires used for the effects of flying. This scene was painted, but some days later at the dress rehearsal he was astonished to see it used as the setting for a short opera which was to precede the ballet. He protested and quarrelled, but without avail. His patience exhausted, he determined to leave Paris; but his friends, promising him success, forced him to remain.

Eventually the ballet was produced on December 12th, 1815, and its reception compensated the weary *maître de ballet* for all his sufferings. It was much admired, and Louis XVIII., who was present, invited Didelot to his box and commanded him to be given a present of 2,000 francs.

But when the composer went to the treasurer he received a bill for expenses amounting to 2,400 francs, so that instead of having money to receive, he owed 400 francs. Didelot paid the account and, though offered a profitable engagement at the Opéra, returned to Russia, being afraid of the omnipotent Gardel.

He was appointed first *maître de ballet*, on the following terms :—

1. The contract to be valid for six years, after which Didelot was to receive a pension, his previous service to be taken into account.

2. The salary for him and his wife to be 16,000 r. per year.
3. Each was to have one benefit a year, at the most favourable period, with all expenses paid by the State.
4. He was to have the use of the theatre carriage, but only when on duty.
5. He was to have a special apartment in the Theatre School, that formerly occupied by the Inspector of the *corps de ballet*.
6. He was to have an annual allowance of 20 *sajen* of wood for fuel.
7. Didelot and his wife were each to have 1,400 r. for their journey to St. Petersburg; the same grant to be allowed them for their return.

In 1816, Didelot returned to St. Petersburg and produced more than twenty ballets. These were *Atys and Galatea* (1816), *The Unexpected Return* (1817), *The Young Dairymaid* (1817), *Carlos and Rosalba* (1817), *The Hungarian Hut* (1817), *Theseus and Ariadne* (1817), *Flore et Zéphyre* (1818), *The Young Girl from the Island* (1818), *Faun and Hamadryad* (revived 1818), and *A Hunting Adventure* (1818, at Hermitage Theatre; the Flemish scene for the second act was reproduced from a painting by Teniers).

Then *The Caliph of Bagdad: A Youthful Adventure of Haroun al Raschid* (1818), a ballet in two acts by M. Didelot, music by Antonolini, fights by Valville, scenery by Conoppi, Martinov and Kondratiev, costumes by Babini. The principal dancers were Mlles. Kolosova and Istomina, and MM. Antonen and Auguste.

Afterwards came *Raoul de Crequis, or The Return from the Crusades*, a grand Pantomimic Ballet in five acts by Didelot, music by Cavos[1] and Sushkov, scenery by Kondratiev and Dranchet, final scene by Conoppi, fights by Gomburov, machines by Burset, costumes by Babini. Principal dancers, Mlle. Kolosova and MM. C. Didelot and Auguste.

[1] Catterino Cavos (born at Venice 1776, died at St. Petersburg April 28th, 1840) was the son of the musical director of the Fenice Theatre. He went to Russia in 1797 as conductor of Astarito's opera company. Two years later he was made director of Italian and Russian operas, and Professor in the Theatre School. He was one of the first composers to give his music a definite national colouring.

Finally, *Hensi and Tao* (1819), *Laura and Henry* (revived 1819), *Charles and Lisbeth* (1820), *Cora and Alonzo* (1820), *Alceste* (1821), *Roland and Morgana* (revived 1821), *The Wooden Leg* (1821), *The Captive of the Caucasus* (1823), *Phædra and Hippolytus* (1825), and *Dido* (1827).

It is difficult to estimate the number of dances produced by Didelot. There was a short one called "The Broken Idol," performed at a benefit for Istomina, in which the youthful Teleshova distinguished herself. He also left a number of *scenarii*, such as *Aeneas and Lavinia, Foolish Head and Kind Heart, The Father's Curse*, and others.

Didelot left the stage in 1829, owing to a quarrel with Prince Gagarin, the director of the theatre. At a certain performance the interval was too long and the Prince commanded the next act to begin earlier and the dancers to be hurried up. Didelot received the order haughtily, and in consequence the Prince threatened him with arrest. The *maître de ballet* gave way, but the next day tendered his resignation, which was accepted.

At this period the romantic ballet was cultivated. In Didelot's ballets there was a theme and dramatic interest; the dances were appropriate to the development of the story, and the miming was expressive. He was never at a loss for an interesting plot, and the creative force and imagination characteristic of his ballets did not fade with time. Some years after his resignation, when he was watching a performance of one of his ballets, there was a call for the composer, and Didelot was much touched by the ovation given him.

He died at Kiev on November 7th, 1837.

During this reign, as a result of Didelot's teaching, many promising Russian dancers were formed. The more important Russian and foreign dancers who appeared during the first quarter of the nineteenth century were as follows:—

Mlles. Kolosova, Birilova, Rosa Colinette (Didelot), Ikonina, Danilova, Novitskaya, Azlova, Saint-Clair, Pleten (afterwards transferred to Moscow), Baptiste, Makhaeva, Istomina, Nikitina, Shemaeva, Likhutina, Osipova, Pimenova, Selezneva, Ovoshnikova, Djianetti, Georges (sister of the famous actress), Zubova, Teleshova, Lobanova and

MARIE TAGLIONI IN "LA FILLE DU DANUBE"
From the lithograph by Razumikhin after the painting by A. Zelensky

Azarevicheva. There were some visiting artistes from Vienna: Mme. Bernadelli and MM. Bernadelli and Urbina.

MM. Didelot, Valberg, Auguste (Poireau), Dutac, Duport, Baptiste, A. Grekov, Lefèvre, Fallet, Léon—the last three were transferred to the Moscow Theatre—André (Schmidt), Antonen, Ebergard, Lustich and Vélange. The last-named made a successful *début* in 1817, and afterwards received a yearly salary of 20,000 r. Then MM. Shelekhov, Shemaev, Striganov, Artemiev, Didier, Goltz, Didelot *fils*, Castillon, Trifonov and many others. Another pupil of Didelot's was A. P. Glushkovsky, who later produced at Moscow several of his ballets.

At this period dramatic artistes often took part in ballets and *vice versâ*. This occurred particularly at benefit performances; for instance, Sosnitsky took the place of Valberg as *premier mime* and danced a Russian dance instead of Auguste.

Evgenia Ivanovna Kolosova, a pupil of Valberg, with beautiful features and a majestic air, was a fine dancer, especially in dramatic dances. Didelot thought her very talented. She appeared at Moscow in 1811 in *Raoul the Bluebeard*, and afterwards astonished everyone by the excellence of her dancing with Auguste. Kolosova took part in the following ballets: *Medea and Jason* (Didelot), *Orpheus and Eurydice* (Valberg), *The Triumph of Russia, or, The Russians in Paris* (Valberg and Auguste), *The Hungarian Hut* and *Raoul de Créquis*.

Marie Nikolaevna Ikonina was a handsome, tall and exquisite dancer. A contemporary declares that in her person were united all the attributes of Diana, Juno and Minerva. Didelot, her teacher, set high hopes on her future. Her dancing was distinguished by its lightness, but she grew so thin that no one would look at her. She danced as Diana in a *pas de deux* with Didelot, as Apollo, in a ballet called *Œdipus*, on December 10th, 1806. In 1809, she danced at Moscow with Novitskaya and Duport. She was also an excellent mime.

Marie Danilova was the muse of a hundred poets and writers. Born in 1795, she was a typical Russian beauty endowed with a lovely body, regular features, sparkling eyes and a smile—to use a phrase of one of her admirers—

that seemed a foretaste of paradise. Her parents had been rich, but a stroke of ill-fortune impoverished the family and caused the dispersion of its members. As Marie was the youngest and prettiest of the children, she was sent to the School of Dancing.

Didelot was her teacher, and he delighted in her good manners and vivacious air, and the interest she displayed in her work. Often he gave her private lessons, for her progress aroused his admiration. She made her *début* at eight years old; but there was nothing stiff or untutored in her movements, they were easy and harmonious.

Satisfied with the applause that greeted her dancing, Didelot withdrew Danilova from the public gaze. He continued to develop her talents and sent her to Kolosova to receive instruction in the art of mime. Only at rare intervals did he permit her to make an appearance, for he did not wish her progress to be retarded by love affairs and social pleasures. Thus she lived for her art alone.

At last Didelot decided that her public career should commence. Her virginal beauty, the grace, precision and ease of her movements procured her a triumph. At once she had scores of admirers, but to all their blandishments she replied: "I am not free, I belong to my art."

But in 1808 the French dancer Duport came to St. Petersburg at the invitation of Didelot. He was accompanied by his mistress, the famous actress Mlle. Georges. At this time her funds were low, and her lover was advancing her money at a high rate of interest, taking her diamonds as security.

Duport made his *début* with Danilova in *Cupid and Psyche*. He was greatly attracted by the beauty of the young dancer, and determined to make her his prize. Being very skilled in this kind of warfare he laid siege; his efforts were soon rewarded with success. He broke off his liaison with Georges and devoted himself to Danilova, who was soon carried away by the joys of her new life.

But in the meantime Georges had also achieved success, and as a result had replenished her coffers. Duport's engagement had nearly run its course, and the crafty dancer, well posted as to Georges's doings, having amassed

EKATERINA TELESHOVA OLGA SCHLEFOCHT AVDOTIA ISTOMINA

200,000 r. and pocketed some of her diamonds, made peace with his former mistress and left Russia, without a single word of farewell to Danilova. The Russian dancer, overcome by such brutal treatment, fell ill. She grew weaker and weaker, and died on January 8th, 1812, at seventeen years old.

Nastasia Semenovna Novitskaya was not beautiful, but had a very amiable manner. In 1809 she danced at Moscow with Duport. Her career was short, and ended sadly. Didelot, to please Count Miloradovich, gave Novitskaya a small part, and the principal one, that should have been hers, to Teleshova. Novitskaya protested, but the Count threatened to have her put in a house of correction. She fell ill, and the Empress Marie Fedorovna sent her own physician to see her. He reported the cause of her illness. At the Empress's command the Count called on Novitskaya, but she was so distressed that she grew worse, and died a few days later. The year was 1822 and she was but twenty-five years old.

The Count Miloradovich appears to have regarded the *corps de ballet* as an institution intended to administer to his personal pleasures. Unfortunately he had considerable influence which he used to gain his ends. He became the director of the school which he transferred to some woods; and soon he had a *Parc des Cerfs* of his own. Like Restif de la Bretonne, he was almost a fetichist in his passion for tiny feet, and when one took his fancy he caused it to be copied in plaster or marble. On one occasion when he ordered Zubova's foot to be modelled, he had a hundred casts made from it.

Avdotia Ilinichna Istomina was the best dancer in the company during the 'twenties. She was a brunette with dark eyes, a little below medium height, easy-going, but somewhat temperamental, and gifted with a charming[1] manner both on and off the stage. Istomina made her *début*

---

[1] The celebrated *ballerina* Thamar Karsavina tells us in her delightful autobiography, *Theatre Street*, of the great impression made upon her, when she was a pupil at the Theatre School, by the portrait of Istomina—" a small, beautiful head in a wreath of roses and nenuphars, with wistful eyes and a smile half lazy, half disdainful "—which stood out from among the engravings of celebrities that covered the walls of the rehearsal room.

on August 30th, 1815, as Galatea in *Atys and Galatea* (Didelot). She also took the part of a Caucasian in *The Captive of the Caucasus*. A most captivating woman, she played a prominent part in the social life of St. Petersburg at this period. Pushkin, who was enamoured of her, describes her dancing in his poem *Evgenia Onegin* :—

> The house is crammed. A thousand lamps
> On pit, stalls, boxes, brightly blaze,
> Impatiently the gallery stamps,
> The curtain now they slowly raise.
> Obedient to the magic strings,
> Brilliant, ethereal, there springs
> Forth from the crowd of nymphs surrounding
> Istomina the nimbly-bounding.
> With one foot resting on its tip
> Slow circling round its fellow swings
> And now she skips and now she springs
> Like down from Ælous's lip,
> Now her lithe form she arches o'er
> And beats with rapid foot the floor
>
> * * *
>
> Shouts of applause ! [1]

V. V. Sheremetev lost his life in a duel on her behalf, and a similar fate nearly overtook another admirer, the dramatist A. S. Griboyedov, who was wounded in another duel.

Istomina died of cholera at Teheran in 1848.

Nathalie Andreyevna Likhutina was noted for the lightness of her dancing and the excellence of her technique. She danced in many of Didelot's ballets, to whom she owed her development: *Atys and Galatea, The Young Girl from the Island, The Hungarian Hut, A Hunting Adventure, A Young Huntress* (Auguste), *Charles and Lisbeth, Raoul de Créquis, The Caliph of Bagdad* and so forth.

Vera Andreyevna Zubova was the school friend of Teleshova and a favourite pupil of Didelot's. She made her *début* in *The Young Dairymaid*. This dancer was a beauty in miniature, being short of stature but perfectly proportioned; she was famed for her tiny feet.

Ekaterina Alexandrovna Teleshova was a *première mime*.

[1] Pushkin (A. S.), *Eugene Onéguine*. Canto I, XVII. Trs. Lt.-Col. Spalding, 1881.

A TAGLIONI DAY AT THE BOLSHOY THEATRE
From the lithograph by R. Zhukovsky

Beautiful and attractive, she was excellent in the following ballets: *The Deserter, Ruslan and Lyudmila, The Return from India*, and *Phædra and Hippolytus*. She also danced in the ballets of Didelot and Auguste. Teleshova died in 1850.

Nadezhda Apollonovna Azarevicheva was also a famous mime. She had irregular features, red hair and small, fiery eyes. This dancer distinguished herself as Hensi in *Hensi and Tao*.

Auguste Poireau, known as Auguste, remained on the stage and became a *maître de ballet*. When Didelot left Russia in 1811, Auguste produced many ballets in conjunction with Valberg.

Dutac was honoured with the position of *premier danseur* during the reign of Alexander I.

Louis Duport, one of the most celebrated French dancers and *chorégraphes*, was born at Paris in 1781. From 1800 he danced in the ballets given at the Théâtre de la Gaité and the Ambigu Comique. He obtained an engagement at the Opéra, then directed by Auguste Vestris. It happened that, owing to the sudden illness of one of the dancers, Duport was given the part of Zephyr in the ballet *Psyche*. The grace, lightness and precision of his dancing achieved such a success, that Vestris at once scented a formidable rival.

The public took sides, and Berchoux made the dispute the subject of a poem called *La Danse, ou la Guerre des Dieux de l'Opéra*. But Vestris pretended to disdain Duport and ridiculed his achievements. Presently, the latter, weary of the struggle, decided to take flight; and one night in May, 1808, he left Paris, disguised as a woman, in company with his mistress, the celebrated actress, Mlle. Georges, and went to St. Petersburg.

At the beginning of his engagement he received 1,200 r. per performance, then a yearly salary of 60,000 r., afterwards increased to 100,000 r. He performed in anacreontic ballets. Duport took part in the ballets *Cupid and Psyche, Flore et Zéphyre, Cupid and Adonis* and *Almaviva and Rosina*. He produced *The Judgment of Paris*. In 1809 he danced with great success at Moscow with Mlles. Saint-Clair, Novitskaya and Ikonina. Duport remained in Russia until February 2nd, 1811, when he danced for the 138th time and received a great ovation.

I. I. Valberg acted mimed rôles until the arrival of Didelot. He produced the following ballets: *The Amazon, Henri IV., Camille* and *The Spirit of Charity*; afterwards, in collaboration with Auguste, he arranged a number of ballets which, though successful, did not attain to the artistry of those of Didelot. Valberg died in 1819 at the age of fifty-three.

Ivan Antonovich Shemaev and Lustich were both appointed to take the place of Duport, but neither succeeded. Shemaev became an efficient pantomimic artiste. Lustich struggled on in the hope of achieving success, and by some was compared to Goltz; but he was neither a Goltz nor a Duport.

André and Didier were both liked in comic parts.

Antonen was noted for his handsome features and the neatness and lightness of his dancing. He danced in an opera-ballet *Télémaque*, the dances for which he composed with Didelot, and the ballets *Carlos and Rosalba, The Young Girl from the Island, Flore et Zéphyre, A Hunting Adventure* and *Phædra and Hippolytus*.

Antonen's place was taken by Vélange who received 20,000 r. per year.

A Parisian dancer, Castillon, who arrived in the 'twenties, achieved a considerable success on the Russian stage. He made his *début* in the ballet *Lisa and Colin*, and received a salary of 18,000 r. He took part in many of Didelot's ballets.

Ivan Ivanovich Ebergard was best known for his dancing of the Mazurka and foreign national dances. He took part in *The Hungarian Hut, The Captive of the Caucasus, Phædra and Hippolytus*, and so on.

N. O. Goltz, who afterwards became one of the greatest of Russian dancers, having completed his training at the Theatre School on February 22nd, 1822, was engaged at a salary of 1,200 r., and for three years received an additional 800 r. annually. He made his *début* in *The Captive of the Caucasus*; he pleased the public and achieved a great success which Istomina shared with him. His talent steadily increased, and later he danced 200 times with Marie Taglioni. Didelot regarded Goltz as particularly excellent in character dancing.

In 1819, a Moscow danseuse, Lobanova, made her *début* in *divertissement*. She partnered an actor, Palnikov, in his gypsy dances. Both were acclaimed by the public for the life and fire of their dancing.

Other eminent dancers of this period were MM. Baptiste, Shelekhov *fils*, Didelot *fils* and Striganov; and Mlles. Lustich, Azlova (who understudied Kolosova in her parts with Didelot), Ovoshnikova, Selezneva and Shemaieva.

The old ballets of Valberg were often produced, and those of Le Picq and Canziani were revived, also several by Auguste and Duport.

When Didelot and Duport went abroad the repertory took on a national patriotic character, which resulted in the production of such ballets as *A Camp Festival, For Love of Country, The Triumph of Russia, or, The Russians in Paris*, which were very successful. These ballets were produced by Auguste and Valberg in collaboration.

From 1816, the ballets of Didelot predominated. At the end of the reign of Alexander, the troupe was formed of the following dancers. Pantomimic parts were acted by E. I. Kolosova, A. T. Azlova, A. A. Shemaeva; *premières danseuses* were: N. A. Lustich, E. A. Teleshova, N. A. Azarevicheva, V. A. Zubova; solo *danseuses* were: M. N. Ikonina, A. O. Nattier, A. I. Lander, then U. A. Selezneva, A. M. Ovoshnikova, K. P. Azarova, T. S. Reutova and A. V. Shcherakova.

C. L. Didelot was the *maître de ballet* and professor of dancing at the Theatre School, Auguste (Poireau) was stage manager and caster of pantomimic parts, which were entrusted to I. A. Shemaev, I. I. Ebergard, André (Schmidt) and P. I. Didier—the last three took comic parts. The *premiers danseurs* were Didelot *fils*, G. I. Striganov and N. O. Goltz. The second dancers were Artemiev and N. T. Trifanov.

From every point the ballets at St. Petersburg reached a high artistic level due to Didelot and his method.

The music for most of the ballets was written by C. Cavos, already mentioned, and Antonolini, the conductor of the Italian opera. Another conductor, Paris, wrote the music for a ballet entitled *L'Arrivée de Thetis;* his pupils Sushkov and Paul Turek also composed ballet music. The latter was an assistant conductor, and the son of Franz Turek, teacher of music in the Theatre School.

Pietro Gonzago continued to be the chief decorative artist, one of his best works being the designs for *Cupid and Psyche*. At one time he was the designer for the theatre at Gatchina. Next in talent were Conoppi, Ivan Martinov, Kondratiev and Louis Dranchet, who designed many settings for ballets and operas.

The performances of the first quarter of the nineteenth century were given in the Bolshoy Theatre, which was burnt down on the night of January 1st, 1811. It was rebuilt by the architect Mauduit on February 3rd, 1818, when it was reopened with a prologue and the ballet *Flore et Zéphyre*.

Many balls took place during the reign of Alexander, who himself excelled in dancing the Mazurka. Among the nobility were many fine dancers, particularly Marie Antonovna Naryshkina (Princess Tchetvertinskaya). The most favoured dances were the Valse, Gavotte, Polonaise, Ecossaise, French Quadrille, Mazurka, and Mazurka with four couples, which was much in vogue from 1814 to 1816.

Dancing became an important part of school studies. For the cadets of the Higher Military School there were both compulsory and voluntary classes directed by Leopold Philippovich Rossi, an old *maître de ballet* aged sixty; he was assisted by Artemiev. The Polonaise and Quadrille were most in favour, while national dances were given every Saturday. The Contredanse or French Quadrille was not yet in vogue, only the simple Quadrille with Valse, Mazurka and Cracoviak. During public examinations different dances were given such as Gypsy, Hungarian and Casatchok.

On November 19th, 1825, the Emperor Alexander died suddenly at Taganrog, while on a visit to the southern governments of his Empire. His reign had resulted in many reforms, and, on the whole, was one of progress. Several universities had been founded, and the condition of the serfs had been bettered. Again, Alexander had acquired enormous prestige as a result of the successful issue of his later wars against Napoleon, but the growing threats to his life due to continual conspiracies and the ever-increasing number of secret societies made his last years sad and unhappy.

MARIE TAGLIONI IN "LA GITANE"
From the lithograph by Blau

PART VIII

UNDER NICHOLAS I.

(1825–1855)

ACCORDING to the law of succession established by Paul in 1797, the heir to the throne was Constantine, born in 1779, who was next in age to Alexander. But he had renounced his claim in 1822, having married Julia Gradzinska, the beautiful daughter of a Polish count. On this basis the throne devolved of right upon Nicholas. He, however, declared the renunciation invalid, and stated that in consequence Constantine was Emperor. It is conjectured that he took up this attitude because he knew of his unpopularity with both public and army. Constantine then made a formal confirmation of the Act of 1822.

On December 12th, the Grand Duke Nicholas consented to accept the throne. But the interregnum, though short, had already given rise to numerous plots. An insurrection broke out in St. Petersburg on the 14th, and there was heavy fighting, but by the evening the revolt was quelled.

The new Emperor was completely different in character from his brother Alexander. He had his good looks, but lacked the other's winning smile and engaging manners which had endeared so many to him. Nicholas was cold without and cold within; not only did his features seem frozen into immobility, but his whole body, his very walk, was stiff and unbending as though his limbs had been sheathed in whalebone.

In some respects he was the first successor to Peter the Great. He was the master and he alone. His ministers and officials were not so much advisers as puppets to make known his wishes and do his bidding. He kept the frontiers close-guarded and bade his subjects occupy themselves with work at home. If they wished to go abroad and visit other countries they must pay for the pleasure by a solid contribution to the taxes. He prohibited books to be imported, and ordered that the French language should be used at Court as little as possible. The faces of his people grew long again.

Yet Nicholas was much interested in the theatre, particularly in the ballet. Often he used to go behind the scenes during the intervals and converse with the artistes. He visited the Imperial Theatre School at least once a year. When the theatrical funds were low the Emperor made up the deficit from his private means, and, in the case of Taglioni and her father, it is a recorded fact that they received from this source alone the sum of 32,000 r. Again, when Elssler arrived he permitted her to make her first appearance at the Court Theatre in Tsarkoe Selo.

In the reign of Nicholas I., ballets were given at the Bolshoy Theatre, except from 1835–36, when the stage and auditorium were being reconstructed. During this period the performances were given first at the Maly Theatre and later at the Alexandrinsky and Mikhaylovsky Theatres; in the summer the performances were held at the Kamennoe-Ostrovsky Theatre, also at the Peterhovsky and Tsarskoe Selsky Theatres. The Alexandrinsky, Kamennoe-Ostrovsky and Mikhaylovsky Theatres were first opened in this reign.

Since the system of entrusting the management of the theatres to a committee was found inconvenient, Prince S. S. Gagarin was appointed Director of Theatres. Unlike his predecessors, he remained faithful to his wife and did not court the dancers.

After a period of mourning lasting nine months, ballet performances were resumed on August 26th, 1826, when a tragedy, *Pozharsky*, was presented. It was followed by a *divertissement, Prince Pozharsky's Return to his Country Estate*, arranged by Auguste. During the Coronation festivities a special repertory was given, consisting of *Hensi and Tao*, *Phædra*, *The Young Dairymaid*, *Raoul de Crequis*, *Carlos and Rosalba* and *Flore et Zéphyre*.

Two years later the company was strengthened by the addition of a new artiste, Marinette Bertrand, but she did not remain long in Russia. Then M. and Mme. Alexis arrived. The former was much liked, for he was a good dancer, though not equal to Goltz. Next, the Parisian dancers Croisette and Paysard were engaged.

Croisette was a well-built girl of twenty, with beautiful features, a good sense of mime and a precise technique. She made her *début* in *Flore et Zéphyre*, but her talents appeared to the best advantage in Titus's ballet *Julius Cæsar in Egypt*, in which she played the part of Cleopatra. She remained in Russia until 1840.

Paysard was married, her husband was the *regisseur* of the French troupe. She had a better *élévation* than Croisette, and her dancing was more tender and voluptuous; but she was not a good mime. She made her *début* in 1832 in *Almaviva and Rosina*. The ballet *Télémaque dans l'Isle de Calypso* was revived for her; in this the part of Cupid was taken by Schlefocht, who afterwards became celebrated. Paysard retired in 1837 as the result of an accident, and died a few years later.

The male side of the company was strengthened by the engagement of the comic dancer Fleury, Frédéric, and Charles Lashouque. The first two were also teachers at the Theatre School. Lashouque was very talented. His powers of miming in particular are said to have been so expressive that the spectator had no occasion to read his programme in order to follow the theme of the ballet. Lashouque danced with Taglioni in several ballets. He was also the first teacher to organise performances of pupils on the school stage; but he did not achieve distinction as a *maître de ballet*.

When Didelot resigned in 1829 as a result of his quarrel with Prince Gagarin, the ballet made no further progress until 1837, the date of the arrival of Marie Taglioni. His place was taken by a new *maître de ballet* called Blache, who came from Bordeaux; at the same time another *maître de ballet*, Titus, was brought from Berlin to act as his assistant.

Soon after Didelot's resignation, the stage manager and dancer Auguste also left the stage. He was succeeded by Ebergard.

Alexis Blache was a son of the well-known dancer and *chorégraphe*, Jean Blache. He was his pupil and succeeded him as *maître de ballet* at Bordeaux in 1820. Previously he had occupied the same position at Marseille. He composed a number of ballets such as *Les Amours d'Automne ou les Vendangeurs* ; *La Dansomanie ou la Fête de M. Balloni* ; *Jean-Jean ou les Bonnes d'Enfants* ; *Les Lauriers d'Ibérie ou la France Victorieuse* ; *Milon de Crotone ou les deux Athlètes* ; *Polichinel vampire* ; *Sylvain ou le Braconnier* ; *Les Meuniers*, etc. His efforts, however, to replace Didelot were unsuccessful. For, though his ballets had been well received abroad, they failed to please the Russian public. Again, he was not a good teacher.

He produced several ballets at St. Petersburg : *Don Juan* ; *Sumbeka, or the Capture of Kazan* ; *Mars and Venus* ; *Love in a Village* ; *Daphnis* ; *Zoraida* ; *Amadis de Gaul* ; and *The Scotsmen*. The best of these were *Mars and Venus* and *Love in a Village*, performed at the opening of the new Mikhaylovsky Theatre.

Titus's work was also received coldly. He is known for his dances to Glinka's *A Life for the Tsar*. But the composer always felt that they did not harmonise with his opera, and in 1843 he asked Goltz to compose a Mazurka which was very successful ; the Krakoviak in this piece was arranged by Didier.

Titus stayed a long while at St. Petersburg. He produced the following ballets : *The Swiss Milkmaid* ; *Kia-King* ; *Julius Cæsar in Egypt* ; *The Virgin Island* ; *The Two Aunts* ; and several of P. Taglioni's ballets such as *La Sylphide*, *La Révolte du Serail* and others. *Kia-King*, *Julius Cæsar in Egypt* and the Taglioni ballets were successful.

In 1834, Auber's opera *La Muette de Portici (Fenella)* was produced at the Alexandrinsky Theatre. Some chorus singers were engaged from Berlin because the opera was produced in German by the German Opera Company at St. Petersburg. The part of the dumb girl was created by K. A. Teleshova, who shared the rôle alternately with M. D. Novitskaya. Teleshova was the better mime, but

ELENA ANDREYANOVA

Novitskaya pleased more, because she was young and pretty, and her performance was simple and natural.

M. D. Novitskaya entered the Theatre School at the age of eight. She made her *début* as Zelia in *A Hunting Adventure*, then appeared in *Flore et Zéphyre* (Didelot). Her teacher was Lustich. After her appearance in *La Muette de Portici* she danced in *Nina, or Driven Mad by Love; The Deserter; Don Juan: The Hungarian Hut*, and others. She was a good mime and danced Russian dances well. In 1835 she married an actor named Dur. This news greatly displeased her admirers, and a hostile party soon formed, determined to show their disapproval. However, the first time she appeared after her marriage, the Emperor was present; but the dread silence that marked her entrance was more pointed than any shouted insults.

The director, Gedeonov, strongly disapproved of marriage between artistes. One day he addressed the pupils on this subject.

"My children, you know nothing of life. And yet, what do I hear? Why, that one of you wishes to be married—and to an actor! What are his means? Have you a dowry? No! Then what are you going to live on? In a year's time you will have children and be unable to dance for several months, and so you will remain all your life in the *corps de ballet*. I really feel sorry for you. You are a nice girl, young and pretty, and ought to gain a fortune."

After her marriage, Novitskaya played old people's parts. In 1839 Dur died, and she decided to become an actress, but she was not successful.

In 1834, another foreign dancer, Gerino, joined the company. He was a clever and expressive dancer, noted for his handsome looks and good manners. Gerino made his *début* in *Daphnis* (Blache), and although the ballet was dull he made his mark. He fell in love with Paysard, who reciprocated his passion, but suspected him of infidelity. In a moment of despair she threw herself out of a window and sustained a broken leg. After this incident Gerino was sent to Moscow, when he was appointed *maître de ballet* and *premier danseur*. He produced many ballets with Mme. Sankovskaya I. Gerino's place was taken by Emile

Gredlu, who afterwards became one of the best teachers at the Theatre School. He made his *début* in *La Sylphide* and was a good partner.

In 1835, the Theatre School was situated in a three-story house facing the Ofitsersky and Ekaterininsky Canals. The older pupils lived on the top floor and were courted by men in the street below. Students and *balletomanes* tried all manner of ways to meet the girls. They endeavoured to creep unnoticed behind the scenes at the theatre; they hid and sought to surprise the girls on their return home. But such incidents were lightly passed over, for the authorities had no wish to embroil themselves with influential parents.

The School staff included two characters: the Doctor, Marochetti, and the Inspector, Solich. The former had one elixir for every ill—a preparation of camphor. The latter, although eighty years old and partly paralysed, wore a flower in his buttonhole as though he were a young man. He always carried a leather thong with which he flicked the rosy cheeks and pretty shoulders of his wards.

In 1836 the school was removed to a site opposite the Alexandrinsky Theatre, when the senior students were transferred to the first floor, but the windows were made of ground glass.

The following year the art of ballet, which had made little progress under Blache and Titus, received a new stimulus due to the promised visit of the celebrated dancer, Marie Taglioni. Her contract with the Paris Opéra having expired on April 25th, she resolved to accept an invitation to appear in Russia. The terms of this contract were very favourable, for she and her father, the *chorégraphe* Philippe Taglioni, were offered the sum of 32,400 r. for the season September to February, and, in addition, she had the right to have three benefits and her father two. To convey an idea of these salaries, it may be stated that the receipts from these special performances generally amounted to 26,000 r.

The famous dancer arrived at St. Petersburg in the autumn of 1837. The foreign newspapers had related the story of her triumphs; some of the St. Petersburg residents had seen her dance when on a visit to Paris, and had brought home glowing accounts of her talent; others had heard of her in letters from acquaintances living abroad.

The first performance, which had originally been fixed for September 3rd, was altered to the 6th, when she danced in *La Sylphide*. This delay only increased the fever of impatience to see her that prevailed. A Russian critic wrote in the *Svernaya Pchela* (Northern Bee) of her performance thus : " Yesterday, September 6th, Marie Taglioni made her *début* in *La Sylphide*, and the public which welcomed her with acclamation and applause was not disappointed in its expectations. Marie Taglioni was recalled at the end of the first act, after her dance in the second act, and three times at the end of the ballet." In his next article the same critic wrote : " The ideal of grace, the ideal of the dance, the ideal of mime—that is Taglioni."[1]

The Bolshoy Theatre, at which she danced, was crowded with the most select audience. The theatre tickets were literally fought for, since to be absent was to forfeit esteem. She was the first dancer in Russia to whom flowers were presented, and the first to be applauded by ladies, who hitherto had regarded such a token of appreciation from their sex as a mark of bad taste.

Even the stern and implacable Emperor melted under the charm of this ethereal vision, and was invariably present whenever she danced. Taglioni's contract was renewed four times, so that she appeared some 200 times. The Emperor had a statue of her placed in the Imperial box, and at one of the early performances he broke all established etiquette by leaving his box and taking a seat in the first row of the stalls, in order to see the stage better.

A. Y. Golovacheva-Panaeva, a former pupil of the Theatre School, gives an interesting impression of Taglioni's arrival. " The most celebrated dancer Taglioni arrived at St. Petersburg with her father and came to our school to do her exercises. The director and the officials treated her with every courtesy. Taglioni was a very plain, excessively thin woman with a small, yellowish and very wrinkled face. I felt quite ashamed because the pupils after the class surrounded Taglioni, and, with a charming note in their voices, said in Russian : ' What an

[1] Quoted Soloviev (N.), *Marie Taglioni*, 1912. p. 32.

ugly mug you've got! How wrinkled you are!' Taglioni, not knowing the language and thinking compliments were being paid to her, smiled and replied in French: 'Thank you, dear children.'"[1]

On November 23rd, 1838, Taglioni appeared for the first time in a new ballet called *La Gitane*. Her partner was N. O. Goltz, who took the rôle of Frédéric. This ballet pleased greatly, especially one dance in which Taglioni as the Gypsy lifted the veil from her face. In addition to the principals, the following dancers also appeared: Mlles. Dur, Teleshova II, Bertrand, Reutova, Ivanova, Samoylova, Shiryaeva, Apollonskaya, and MM. Lashouque, Frédéric, Shelikhov I, Artemiev, Goltz, Fleury and Spiridonov.

When *La Gitane* was announced, thousands of persons stood at the entrance to the theatre from early morning. After the performance the dancer became so popular that all kinds of articles were named after her. There were Taglioni caramels, Taglioni cake, *coiffures à la* Taglioni, and so forth.

When the dancer fell ill, the capital was in despair. The *Svernaya Pchela* for December 9th reported: "Taglioni has been ill for two whole weeks, and all this time Petersburg has been suffering from spleen. Other artistes try to divert the public, but all in vain."

On January 16th, 1839, Taglioni created a new furore. She appeared in a blue satin sarafan and danced a Russian dance.

On November 28th of the same year, she appeared in *L'Ombre*, a ballet by her father with music by Maurer. A contemporary declared that Taglioni's resemblance to a shadow was perfect. "It is impossible to describe the suggestion she conveyed of aerial flight, the fluttering of wings, soaring in the air, alighting on flowers and gliding over the mirror-like surface of a river." This ballet was lavishly mounted with scenery by Fedorov, Serkov, Shenian, and Roller; the dresses were designed by Mathieu. The dancers were Mlles. Smirnova, Andreyanova and Schlefocht, and MM. Gredlu and Lashouque. Taglioni, Apollonskaya and Goltz appeared in a *pas de trois* in the third act.

Other ballets in which Taglioni appeared during her

[1] Quoted Pleshchayev, *op. cit.*, p. 101, also Soloviev, *op. cit.*, pp. 37, 38.

ELENA ANDREYANOVA
Medal struck in her honour at Milan, circa 1846

visits to Russia (1837–1842) were *La Fille du Danube, La Bayadère Amoureuse, Le Corsaire, Le Lac des Fées, L'Elève d'Amour, Dya,* and *Gerta.* The last-named was noted for an Aragonese dance with castanets, and a *pas de deux* by Taglioni and Johannsen.

Taglioni did not stray from St. Petersburg. There were overtures from Moscow, but as the dancer demanded 3,000 r. per performance and a benefit in addition, nothing came of them.

How did Taglioni dance? Gousse says: " She danced like a goddess not on, but rather over, the stage. She seemed to be included in the company of Diana's nymphs, she never could have taken part in the dances of Venus. She always lived for her art so that earthly cares did not trouble her. Thus her admirers were not old men sitting in the first rows of the stalls or students come from boarding schools without permission. The expression of her eyes was meek and modest, not fiery. Her smile and poses were not provocative as if she desired admiration, because she radiated a certain saintliness. She was a smiling, ethereal beauty appealing to the mind and not to the senses."[1]

The great dancer held her farewell benefit performance on January 26th, 1842, when she appeared in *Yetta, Reine des Elfrides.* During her last week she danced each day one of her old ballets; this revival of old memories made still sadder the thought of her approaching departure. The official last performance was given on March 1st on the Sunday before Lent, and was particularly ceremonious. Taglioni was recalled before the curtain eighteen times. Moved to tears by this demonstration of affection the dancer came to the edge of the stage and said: " *Eternellement, vous serez gravés dans mon cœur, et si je fais mes adieux à la Russie, ce n'est pas pour toujours.*"

But the public could not part with its favourite so quickly, and hence two more performances were given in the first week in Lent for " the benefit of dissenters," as they were styled in the newspapers. The public's enthusiasm was unbounded because each member of the audience felt that he was seeing the dancer for the last time. She was recalled thirty times and again made her speech, but this

[1] Quoted Pleshchayev, *op. cit.*, p. 106.

time in German; "*Empfangen Sie meinen herzlichsten Dank. Ich hoffe dass ich zurück kommem werde.*" This promise to return,[1] however, was never kept and her departure left a void which it seemed could never be filled.

In the middle of March an advertisement in the *Vyedomostey S.-Peterburgsky Politsii* announced that, owing to the immediate departure of Mme. Taglioni, the contents of her house—furniture, bronzes, plate, services, cutlery, and so on—would be sold by public auction. On the day of the sale the house was crowded with buyers eager to secure a souvenir of the dancer. It is said that a pair of her shoes was purchased for 200 r. They were then cooked, served with a special sauce, and eaten at a dinner organised by a group of *balletomanes*.

The most prominent Russian dancers at this period were Schlefocht, Andreyanova, Smirnova and Johannsen. The successive seasons of Taglioni greatly aided the development of their talents.

Olga Timofeyevna Schlefocht was born at St. Petersburg in 1822, and appeared first in 1833, when the Mikhaylovsky Theatre was opened, in the ballet *L'Amour à la Campagne*. Later she danced with Taglioni, whom she studied closely. She followed her every movement, studied her style, admired her grace, and incidentally improved herself. Schlefocht was much liked, and it was expected that she would become a celebrated dancer, but she developed consumption and died.

Tatiana Petrovna Smirnova was born in 1821 and entered the Theatre School in 1827, where she studied dancing, first under Didelot, later with Mme. Lustich and Titus. In 1828 she performed the rôle of Cupid in *Flore et Zéphyre*. It is stated that for her dancing in a *pas de cinq* from *La Fille du Danube* at the time of Taglioni's first visit, and for the *Bolero* and *Tyrolienne* dance she performed with the famous dancer, she received many handsome presents from the Court.

---

[1] It would appear that Taglioni's promise to return was a diplomatic falsehood employed to soften the pain of parting, for in a letter dated January 5/17, 1842, written from St. Petersburg, and addressed to a friend, M. Courtin, the dancer states: "Je quitte la Russie au mois de mars pour sans doute n'y plus revenir." (See *La Revue Musicale*. Special Number for December, 1921, p. 129.)

After Taglioni's departure, Smirnova performed many of her celebrated parts. Her talent developed under Taglioni's influence. She took all she could from her, so that her dancing became a successful imitation of the model. She was modest, shy, and executed all her movements with care. Her chief quality was an extreme lightness which showed in all her work. She danced without visible effort, and, in fact, seemed to have been destined to fly among the *corps de ballet*. The public preferred her to all others, and the Director of the Imperial Theatres encouraged her success. The second year after she left school she was allowed a benefit, an unprecedented honour. In 1844, she was granted leave of absence and danced abroad. She married a M. Nevakhovich.

Elena Ivanovna Andreyanova was born in 1819 and entered the Theatre School on April 10th, 1837. Like Smirnova, she performed many of the parts associated with Taglioni. In this connection, Zotov wrote:

"When Taglioni left us, the public became despondent. All these beautiful ballets were like orphans, pitied, but not consoled. And what do we see? Mme. Andreyanova has decided to perform all those different, gigantic parts. I regret to say that the public, still saddened by Taglioni's departure, did not realise our dancer's feat, and the theatre remained empty.

"Some people thought that Andreyanova wished to prove that she was Taglioni's equal. Others did not wish to see the ballets in which Taglioni had delighted them. But both parties were wrong. Andreyanova deserved the public's thanks and sympathy. She did not wish to equal Taglioni, but to prove that a Russian dancer need not fail in a part performed by the best European talent.

"As the outcome of her efforts and application she attained a high degree of talent, and used all her powers to support our ballet, which she did with a rare art. *La Gitane*, *Le Lac des Fées*, *Gerta* and *Le Corsaire*—all these difficult and immense parts she performed excellently. Little by little her work came to be appreciated, and it could not be gainsaid that her accomplishments entitled her to admiration even from those who had seen Taglioni."[1]

[1] Quoted Pleshchayev, *op. cit.*, p. 111.

A new development increased her success. The director, seeing that the memory of Taglioni made the position of the dancers difficult, sent the *maître de ballet* to Paris with a commission to bring back a new ballet. This was an excellent plan, and led to the presentation in Russia on December 18th, 1842, of the ballet *Giselle* (theme by Coralli and T. Gautier, music by A. Adam).

Andreyanova performed the title rôle, and, since she could not be compared with anyone, everyone realised that she was quite competent to perform a Taglioni part. The new ballet was well executed. Andreyanova's miming in the first act and her dancing in the second proved that she was the first dancer in Russia. She was likewise excellent in character dancing. Her celebrated Saltarello, with its mingled poetry, charm and voluptuousness, could rouse to frenzy the most jaded spectator.

Andreyanova was much favoured by Gedeonov, who ordered her to be protected from the officers and *balletomanes* who waited outside the school. A. Y. Golovacheva-Panaeva states that Andreyanova was served with a special dinner and expensive wines at the school, and that Gedeonov ordered the same fare to be served to Smirnova. When the former left the school, she did not use her influence to harm other dances, but her position made her many enemies. At this time all the ballets were produced for her, which raised protests from the public and the admirers of other dancers.

According to other sources these protests had some ground for their being, because Andreyanova tried to intrigue against both Taglioni and Smirnova. The public organised scenes and often hissed her. As a result, in 1844, she was ordered to go to Moscow, where her foot became sore, and for seven weeks she was unable to appear on the stage.

On March 21st, 1845, Andreyanova obtained permission to go abroad without her salary being forfeited. The first time her application was refused, the second time it was granted. She asked to be allowed a period of leave to enable her to rest her foot, with permission to dance at foreign theatres, like Smirnova and the Moscow dancer Sankovskaya. She had the offer of a profitable engagement

CHRISTIAN JOHANNSEN

at the Hamburg Theatre and insisted that the rest and change of air would restore her to health.

J(ules). J(anin)., in the *Journal des Débats* for December 15th, 1845, describes her appearance at Paris in October: " Mlle. Andreyanova, then, the St. Petersburg *première danseuse*, is a light and agile dancer, with a pretty turn of head which recalls Mlle. Taglioni in her youth. It is easy to see that she loves her art and realises its importance to the full. We do not know whether she is a favourite pupil of Taglioni's, but we were soon conscious of that indescribable mixture of artlessness and boldness which contributed so much to the Sylphide's classic charm. Mlle. Andreyanova danced three times. At first she trembled like a Russian birch-leaf, but the favourable reception our public accorded her restored her confidence. At her second appearance she was greeted with unanimous applause. Finally, on the third day, she received an encore for her spirited performance of a charming mazurka. Then the young dancer was recalled with bravos and flowers. She was deemed equal to a Parisienne. On these days the Opéra might almost be said to have resembled a diplomatic reception. In fact, for the Russians, it was as though their national honour was at stake, as the honour of France was at Fontenoy, when the *Gardes-françaises* opposed to the English cried : " You fire first, gentlemen."

Later, Andreyanova went to Milan, where a special medal was struck in her honour.

At St. Petersburg, in the 'forties, ballet was given on Mondays, Wednesdays and Fridays. At the Bolshoy Theatre the season began at the end of Easter and concluded on the second day of Lent the following year. At that time the custom of giving ballet in summer had not been abolished, for though many residents spent that season in the country, many other people came to St. Petersburg and many regiments were transferred to the capital.

The performances at the Bolshoy Theatre were very crowded. Long rows of carriages stretched past both sides of the theatre, and the drivers and postillions sat at fires in the street in winter, or played cards in summer.

At the ballet the first rows of seats were occupied by old, highly-placed officials, but here and there could be found

E

some youthful *balletomane* who shouted "Bravo!" or "*C'est charmant.*" The second and third rows were generally not fully occupied until after the second or third acts, when these seats were taken by the spectators in the distant rows. Often those in the first rows changed to the back rows where the artistes who were not dancing were seated, exchanging notes and talking scandal. The third tier of boxes was occupied by the girl pupils of the Theatre School, and not seldom the sight of the long row of girls in light blue dresses and white capes attracted the attention of the audience more than the stage. Some of the *balletomanes* had small spy-glasses which were just then coming into vogue.

The boxes near the stage were generally occupied by *balletomanes* who in some respects differed from the present ones. The old *balletomane*, while nearly always courting some dancer, successively fell in love with each one that appeared on the stage. And if he paid particular attention to one, that did not prevent his admiring others and patronising them all. He knew the history of every dancer and the gossip respecting her, even to those in the last line of the *corps de ballet*.

After the performance he waited at the stage door until the dark green carriages used for the conveyance of the junior artistes drove up, then he looked out particularly for one shaped like a Noah's Ark and called *lineka*. To see this carriage off was the pleasure and duty of every *balletomane*. Outside the theatre they met each other in different *cafés* and restaurants. They had oysters at Izler's, steaks at the Domenique, and champagne at the Béranger. The restaurant especially patronised by *balletomanes* was the Nord in the *Ofitsersky*.

Later in the year 1847, Andreyanova was ordered to Moscow, and both Petipas went with her to produce *Paquita* and *Le Diable Amoureux*. At the old capital there was a celebrated *danseuse* called E. A. Sankovskaya. She had been trained under Taglioni's influence and had remained faithful to her. When Andreyanova appeared in *Giselle* on October 22nd she was well received by the Moscow public, but the supporters of Sankovskaya did all in their power to hinder her success. They hissed her, and on

December 5th a great scandal took place. During the first act of *Paquita*, immediately after the Saltarello had been danced by Andreyanova and M. Montessu, and encored, a dead cat was thrown on the stage; attached to its tail was a label bearing the inscription *première danseuse*. The performance was stopped, but the spectators rose to their feet and excitedly called for Andreyanova. She consented to appear to the public, but refused to dance.

The dancer was received with tremendous applause. Every spectator wished to prove that she had offended one man only and that all respected her talent and admired her. She was recalled three times, then the performance was continued. During the final *entr'acte* the indignation of the artistes rose to such a pitch that they wished to demonstrate to Andreyanova their regret at such an incident. When the curtain was lowered, all the artistes went on the stage, and when Andreyanova appeared they shouted "Bravo!" and kissed her hands to show their affection. At the same time the audience applauded vigorously for Andreyanova to appear. The curtain was raised and they witnessed the scene that was taking place behind. She was recalled a second and a third time, when all the artistes again went on to the stage and applauded her in the presence of the public. Later P. A. Bulgakov confessed himself the culprit.

On her return from Moscow, Andreyanova appeared in *L'Elève des Fées, A Wilful Wife, The Naiad and the Fisherman* —all by Perrot—and *Vert-Vert*, by Mazilier, in which she danced with Elssler and Grisi. She had an excellent success as a mime and as a character dancer. Andreyanova is buried at Paris in the cemetery of Père-Lachaise, not far from where Balzac sleeps. At the base of the tomb is the simple inscription: "HÉLÈNE ANDRIANOFF, *Décédée le* 26 *Octobre*, 1857."

One of the most distinguished members of the male personnel was Christian Petrovich Johannsen. He was born at Stockholm on May 20th, 1817, and received his training at the Stockholm Theatre School. In 1836 he made his *début* at the Royal Theatre. Then, at the expense of the heir apparent, Prince Oscar, he was sent to Copenhagen to study under Bournonville, who praised his abilities and found him a worthy pupil. Mention has been made of his first appearance at St. Petersburg on May 31st, 1841, with Andreyanova in a *pas de deux* in *La Gitane*.

In his youth he was very elastic, graceful and light. His every movement was rounded and his work in classical ballet was distinguished for its fine style. He rendered the most valuable services to the Imperial Ballet both as dancer and teacher. In 1884 he retired from the stage, but continued as professor at the Theatre School, where he taught the young artistes from 1869. He celebrated his fifty years' jubilee on December 8th, 1891.

In January, 1843, a young and beautiful Danish dancer, Lucile Grahn, made her *début* in *Giselle*. At first she was received coldly, despite her beautiful performance in the scene of madness and death. Not until the second act did she conquer the audience by her dances, when she was applauded as much as Taglioni. But after two appearances she became ill and her performances were cancelled.

Grahn was born at Copenhagen on June 30th, 1821, and was the daughter of a former officer. She entered the Royal School of Dancing in 1828, and in 1835 made a successful *début* in *La Muette de Portici (Fenella)*. Then she went to Paris, where she studied under Barrez and made her first appearance at the Opéra on July 12th, 1839, in Mozart's *Don Juan*. She also danced in *Le Carnaval de Venise* and *La Somnambule*, but, unable to make headway against Taglioni, she went abroad. In 1844 she appeared at London, and in April of the following year achieved a striking success in *Eoline*. Three months later she danced with Taglioni, Cerrito and Grisi in the famous *Pas de Quatre*, and in 1848, also at London, appeared with Taglioni and Cerito in the *Pas des Déesses* in *Le Jugement de Paris* arranged by Perrot. Grahn died at Munich in 1907.

On October 1st, *The Miller*, a ballet arranged by E. Gredlu, which had pleased Gedeonov when produced on the school stage, was given at the Mikhaylovsky Theatre. At the end of the year, Titus produced *The Enchanters*, a comic ballet in one act. At the beginning of 1847 he produced another new ballet, *The Talisman and the Dancer*, the principal dancers being Mlles. Yakovleva, Richard and Prikhunova, and M. Johannsen.

LUCILE GRAHN
From the lithograph by H. Grevedon

This year is an important one in the history of the Russian ballet, since it marks the arrival of Marius Petipa.

Marius Ivanovich Petipa, the son of the *maître de ballet* Jean Petipa, was born at Marseille on March 11th, 1822. When sixteen years old he danced at Paris in a *pas de deux* with Grisi, on the occasion of the benefit given for Rachel at the Comédie Française. Later he danced at the Grand Opéra when a benefit was given for Fanny Elssler. Then he went to Nantes, where he was engaged as dancer and *maître de ballet*. In the latter capacity he produced during 1838: *Le Droit du Seigneur, La Petite Bohémienne* and *La Noce à Nantes*. His next engagement was as *premier danseur* at Bordeaux, where he remained for three years and devised several ballets: *La Jolie Bordelaise, La Vendange, L'Intrigue Amoureuse*, all in 1841; and *La Langage des Fleurs* in 1842. He then went to Madrid where he produced five new ballets: *La Fleur de Grènade* (1843), *La Perle de Seville, L'Aventure d'une Fille de Madride* (1844), *Départ pour les Courses de Taureaux* (1845), and *Carmen et son Torero* (1846), and danced at various theatres with the *danseuse* Guy St. Stephan. He studied the native dances with great care, and employed his knowledge to good purpose when he produced ballets in Russia.

Marius's brother, Lucien, was *premier danseur de demi-caractère* at the Opéra, Paris, and having made Titus's acquaintance when the latter was on a visit to the capital, he wrote him a letter asking him to recommend his brother as a dancer for the St. Petersburg stage. Titus discussed the matter with Gedeonov, and replied: " Your brother has been engaged; you may consider this letter as equivalent to a contract." So Marius went to St. Petersburg, where he arrived on May 24th. The next day he reported himself to Gedeonov, who inquired:

" Did you have a pleasant voyage ? "

" Yes, Your Excellency; and when shall I make my first appearance ? "

" Never mind that, my dear; go for a walk and have a rest."

" But, Your Excellency, I am engaged."

" Quite so, but go for a walk."

" But I have no money."

"Well, you can have an advance if you wish. Take a rest for three months and visit our islands; they are very charming."

"It is very strange to be given money and told to take a rest."

"Yes, but there are no performances until August, and you will make your *début* at the beginning of the winter season."

"This is a fine country," replied Petipa; "they tell you to take a rest, and pay you money for doing so."

Petipa made his first appearance in *Paquita* and *Le Diable Amoureux*. He was appointed *premier danseur*, and replaced Emile Gredlu.

In October, 1848, there arrived at St. Petersburg, quite unexpectedly, the celebrated Fanny Elssler. A fortnight later there was another arrival, the *maître de ballet* Jules Perrot.

Elssler had already written twice to the direction expressing her desire to dance at St. Petersburg for a series of performances, but having received no answer she decided to come in person. It would seem that Gedeonov, the protector of Andreyanova, did not wish her to be pitted against Elssler, and so, by ignoring her letters, had thought to be rid of her. Her sudden arrival filled him with consternation. He could not refuse to receive so celebrated a dancer, but explained that his funds were very low, so low that he could not offer the great artist more than 3,000 r. and two half-benefits. To his astonishment, Elssler accepted the terms.

The Emperor, learning of Elssler's arrival, commanded Gedeonov to invite her to dance at the Court Theatre at Tsarkoe Selo. The director was much disconcerted, for it was his duty to make all the necessary arrangements and to be present at the rise of the curtain. Elssler appeared in a Spanish costume and danced her famous *Cachuca*. The Emperor, a little surprised by the passion of her dancing, gradually fell under its charm. He applauded, and his suite did likewise, including the distracted Gedeonov, who saw that Andreyanova's star was threatened.

Franziska Elssler, called Fanny, was born at Vienna on June 23rd, 1810. Her father, Jean Florian Elssler, was valet and copyist to the composer Haydn; her mother was a Viennese embroideress. Fanny made her first appearance at the Kærnthner-Thor when seven years old. She studied under Aumer. An Italian impresario, Barbaja, who brought an Italian troupe to Vienna in 1822, was much impressed by the little girl's dancing, and with the parents' permission took her to Italy, where she studied sometimes at the Scala, Milan, and sometimes at the San Carlo Theatre, Naples.

She returned to Vienna in 1827, and three years later went to Berlin, where she made her *début* in *Nathalie ou La Laitière Suisse*. After several appearances alternately at Vienna and Berlin, she went to London in May, 1833, where she was well received. Thence she went to Paris, and on September 15th, 1834, made her *début* at the Opéra in *La Tempête*, her performance as Alcine being much praised. In 1836 she made her first big success as Florinde in *Le Diable Boiteux*, produced on June 1st, in which she danced the *Cachuca* ever afterwards to be associated with her.

The poet and critic, Théophile Gautier, gives a delightful picture of the dancer: "She comes forward in her pink satin *basquine* trimmed with wide flounces of black lace; her skirt weighted at the hem fits tightly over her hips; her slender waist boldly arches and causes the diamond ornament on her bodice to glitter; her leg, smooth as marble, gleams through the frail mesh of her silk stocking; and her little foot at rest seems but to await the signal of the music. How charming she is with her big comb, the rose behind her ear, her lustrous eyes and her sparkling smile! At the tips of her rosy fingers quiver ebony castanets. Now she darts forward; the castanets begin their sonorous chatter. With her hands she seems to shake down great clusters of rhythm. How she twists, how she bends! What fire! What voluptuousness! What precision! Her swooning arms toss about her drooping head, her body curves backwards, her white shoulders almost graze the ground. What a charming gesture! Would you not say that in that hand which seems to skim the dazzling barrier of the footlights, she gathers up all the desires and all the enthusiasm of the spectators?"

The same writer describes the dancer's appearance

thus: "*La* Fanny is tall, beautifully formed, with limbs that strongly resemble the hunting Diana, combining strength with the most delicate and graceful style. Her small and classically shaped head is placed on her shoulders in a singularly elegant manner; the pure fairness of her skin requires no artificial whiteness, while her eyes beam with a species of playful malice, well-suited to the half-ironical expression at times visible in the corners of her finely-curved lips. Her rich, glossy hair, of bright chestnut hue, is usually braided over a forehead formed to wear, with equal grace and dignity, the diadem of a queen, or the floral wreath of a nymph."

As a dancer, Gautier says: "Mlle. Elssler has strength, precision, a simplicity of gesture, firm *pointes*, a petulant and arch boldness, altogether Spanish, and a serene and happy ease in everything she does which makes her dancing one of the most delightful things in the world to watch—moreover, she has what Taglioni lacks, a profound sense of the dramatic; she dances as well as her rival, and acts better."

On April 14th, 1840, Elssler left for America on a short tour which, originally planned for a few weeks, actually lasted for two years. Her appearance was everywhere marked by the most extraordinary enthusiasm. On her return she gave a series of performances at Berlin, which began on October 28th, 1842, with *Le Dieu et la Bayadère*. She went to London the following year and again in 1847. In 1844–1845 she visited Buda Pesth, and made a series of tours in Italy until 1848. The next four years she went to Russia. On June 21st, 1851, she gave her farewell performance at Vienna in the ballet *Faust*. Having retired from the stage, she lived happily in the town of her birth, loved and respected, until her death on November 27th, 1884.

Elssler made her Russian *début* at the Bolshoy Theatre on October 10th, in *Giselle*. But she was not suited to supernatural parts, and at first her reception was cold, but the dramatic intensity of her miming in the death scene was received with unanimous applause. At this time she was no longer young, but she had retained all her grace and precision of movement. Her body was supple, her dancing vigorous, yet ever distinguished by a captivating grace that

FANNY ELSSLER IN "LE DIABLE BOITEUX"
From the lithograph by A. Lakoshy

could not be withstood. The Russian critics thought her technique inferior to Taglioni's, but when Elssler danced she stirred her audience to a frenzy, and the impression persisted for days. As one critic said : " Taglioni symbolises the ether ; Elssler, earth mingled with fire." [1]

During the winter season five ballets were produced: *Le Rêve du Peintre, La Fille Mal Gardée, Esmeralda* and *Catherine ou la Fille du Bandit*. Afterwards she took part in a drama by Scribe—*Yelva, ou l'Orpheline Russe*, and danced character dances in different ballets.

Le Rêve du Peintre was produced by the dancer herself. A Russian critic, Koni, declares that Elssler's mime was simple, unaffected and readily understood. This ballet concerns a painter who creates his idea of beauty and then falls in love with his work ; but he meets a girl who is the personification of his ideal. Elssler as Lise achieved a triumph. A *balletomane* who saw both Elssler and Virginia Zucchi (a *prima ballerina* of later days) in this part compared them thus : " Zucchi was very ingenious in the emotional scenes, but Elssler surpassed her for artlessness, coquetry and gaiety."

Perrot's ballets *Esmeralda* and *Catherine* gave Elssler splendid opportunities for displaying her art. In the first-named the cast was as follows : Didier (*Quasimodo*), J. Perrot (*Gringoire*), Goltz (*Claude Froleau*). Elssler's miming was so affecting in the scene where Esmeralda bids Gringoire farewell and goes to the scaffold, that many spectators shed tears. She was also much admired as Catherine, the chieftainess of the *banditti*, particularly in the musket dance, one of Perrot's masterpieces.

The following season, Elssler appeared in the same ballets and also in some new ones—*Nathalie ou La Laitière Suisse, Le Tarentule* and *L'Elève des Fées*. The first, by Taglioni, Gyrowetz and Caraja, was withdrawn after two performances. *Le Tarentule*, by Coralli, is an opera worked into a ballet. The biting of a tarantula is followed by a madness which makes the victim run round and round. The theme was only suitable for a comic dance, yet it was strung out to fill two acts. Nevertheless, though dull, it achieved a measure of success.

[1] *Annuaire Dramatique de la Belgique* for 1844.

L'Elève des Fées was reminiscent of Didelot's ballets. Perrot as Aline gave a wonderful display of his ability to mime, and Elssler's dancing was much admired. In the same ballet Andreyanova attained success as the Black Fairy.

Elssler was a great favourite with her fellow artistes and often gave her services at benefits for Russian artistes. One day, when visiting the Theatre School, Elssler singled out Muravieva—who afterwards became celebrated —and said: " She will succeed me." Elssler was very hospitable, and after every performance asked her admirers to take tea with her, but instead of tea she provided a splendid supper.

When she visited Moscow in 1850 her reception was at first indifferent, but it was not long before the Moscow *balletomanes* began to outdo the Americans in the extravagance of their demonstrations. They took the horses from her carriage and pulled her home. They laid carpets before the door of her house, rained flowers on her and cried: " *Hourra !* " In 1851 she again danced at Moscow, and on March 2nd she gave her farewell performance.

In this connection it is of interest to cite an article in the *Moskvitian*, by N. V. Berg, entitled *Good-Bye* :

" Moscow is attracted only by ballets, although the prices are higher. The Bolshoy Theatre is now overcrowded each time the celebrated Fanny Elssler dances. Her contract will end very soon, but it is not our old capital, but the whole of Europe that will be deprived of her talent, because Elssler has said that she will end her career at Moscow, with the exception of some farewell performances she intends to give at Vienna, at which town she began her career. This shows the depth of her wisdom. Like Rubini, she does not wish to outlive her glory, but to lay down Terpsichore's sceptre while her art is in full bloom. She leaves the stage when every theatre regards her as the supreme artist. All the connoisseurs exclaim sadly : ' But why does Elssler wish to leave the stage ? She could replace Taglioni, but who could replace her ? ' These arguments are not unfounded, because there is no dancer in Europe who can boast such lightness, such strength, such beauty and such grace ; Elssler has all those qualities, and even Time has touched her lightly. See her in *La Fille Mal Gardée*. Would you give her more than eighteen years? My feeble pen cannot write a panegyric. So much has been written in Europe and America. See her dance a Saltarello, a Tarantella, a Russian dance, a Casatchok, and you would swear that she had been born, educated and grown up at Naples, or Spain, or Russia, or Little Russia, because the spirit and manners of those peoples are so well expressed by her."[1]

The day before the last performance the Russian and French artistes assembled at a *matinée* at which *Catherine* was being performed. They went to Elssler's dressing-room and sent one of their number to ask Fanny to come and see them. The dancer came attired as Catherine. A. T. Saburova then offered her, on behalf of the artistes of the Imperial Theatre of Moscow, a bracelet with these two inscriptions: *A Fanny Elssler, les artistes de Moscou—Au cœur le plus noble, au talent le plus beau*. The artiste Lensky read a poem in Russian, and afterwards Oudinot, the stage manager of the French troupe, read a translation prepared by the French artiste Moreau:

A l'incomparable Fanny Elssler

Qui voudrait mettre à prix un talent si charmant,
Trouverait-il au monde un égal diamant ?
Dans trois simples joyaux notre offrande s'exprime :
Reconnaissance, amour, inaltérable estime.

Fanny's eyes filled with tears, and she replied with a simple "*merci*," which was followed by cries and kisses. Then she put the bracelet on her arm and repeatedly kissed it during the performance.

The following day came the last performance. The seats at the Petrovsky Theatre were sold for fabulous sums. The ballet chosen was *Esmeralda*. No sooner did the dancer make her entrance than she was almost overwhelmed by a rain of bouquets from every part of the house, many of them adorned with costly lace. Then Prince Galitsin, on behalf of the people of Moscow, offered the artist a large bouquet of white camelias and a silver gilt box in the form

[1] Quoted Pleshchayev, *op. cit.*, pp. 132, 133.

of a *kalatch*. Elssler opened the box and found inside salt and a rich gold bracelet set with six precious stones—Malachite, Opal, Sapphire, Chalcedony, Venissa,[1] Amethyst—the first letter of whose names in Russian spelt the name of Moscow in Russian—Москва (Moskva). This bracelet cost 3,000 r., the proceeds of a subscription organised by Prince Galitsin. Elssler shed tears, put the bracelet on her arm and kissed it.

All the spectators, young and old, men and women alike, began to cry out of sympathy for the celebrated dancer at this, the greatest moment of her career. Fanny, overcome with emotion, knelt down, took off the bracelet and slowly and gracefully kissed each of the six stones. Spectators, artistes, even the members of the orchestra became one in the universal feeling of sadness at the thought of Fanny's approaching departure.

The tense atmosphere was not without its effect on Elssler's dancing. According to an eye-witness, the Countess Rostopchin: "Fanny, electrified, carried away, danced as never before; she did marvellous, almost superhuman things. For instance, she remained *en attitude sur la pointe* for nearly three minutes. At another moment, supported by Théodore, with one mighty leap she rose as high as the dancer's head and yet all her movements seemed effortless. Not for one moment did she lose her customary lightness, her never-failing grace. She rose, vaulted, pirouetted, joyous and flamboyant, fleet and elated, sustained by the general inspiration, carried away by the universal enthusiasm. That moment will never be forgotten by those who were present. Nothing can compare with the fragrance of that supernatural affection which dominated all of us so strongly. No artiste, even the most admired, no matter when or where, has ever been so honoured before."[2] During the performance Elssler received forty-two calls!

There is another description, by Prince Engalytchev, in the *Teatralny Mirok*, 1844. "During the first act, 300 bouquets were thrown on the stage. In the second act the sofa for Esmeralda was made of these flowers, with a large

[1] A kind of garnet.

[2] Quoted Ehrhard (A.) *Une Vie de Danseuse : Fanny Elssler*, 1909, pp. 398, 399.

JULES PERROT AND CARLOTTA GRISI IN "ESMERALDA"
From the lithograph by J. Bouvier

bouquet instead of a cushion placed upon it. This act begins with the scene when Esmeralda, dreaming of her beloved Phœbus, writes his name on the wall. In performing this part the artiste usually pretends to write and then a small, lettered board is shown. Elssler, however, always wrote the word with chalk, in Russian, but that evening she wrote Москва (Moskva) as if to show how she liked this hospitable town. Her action was received with an unheard-of ovation. In the course of my life I have seen many celebrities from Grisi to Vazem, but none of them can be compared to Elssler. Some had a few points of resemblance: Ferraris, Muravieva and Vazem in their technique; M. S. Petipa and d'Or in their *plastique*; Lebedeva in her miming. In the latter respect Elssler surpassed all the celebrities. When you saw her, you felt it to be a pity that she was not an actress, for she would have been another Rachel or Ristori."

Such a combination of talents as Elssler and Perrot, who were surrounded by many brilliant artistes, aided the Imperial Ballet to attain a high reputation. Perrot made the ballet an expression of the theme so that the dances corresponded to a drama in choregraphy. The scenes with the *corps de ballet* were conceived in a rare and beautiful *plastique*. Perrot's compositions were reminiscent of Didelot, but while the latter surpassed Perrot in creative power, the former gave his works a more poetic *mise en scène*. In short, Didelot's ballets seemed almost crude in comparison with those of Perrot. This, however, does not diminish Didelot's talent, it simply marks the development of æsthetic taste. Perrot's determination to develop the mimetic side of ballet was supported by every admirer, especially after the experiments of Blache and Titus, who relied on theatrical effect for the success of their ballets.

Perrot proved himself to be an artist from his first two productions: *Esmeralda* (1848) and *Catherine* (1849). Each represented a complete unity of very unusual dances with mimed drama, and contained many scenes of dramatic interest. When composing his ballets, Perrot considered his whole company, from the *prima ballerina* to the youngest recruit in the *corps de ballet*, and tried to give each one an opportunity to distinguish herself.

Jules Joseph Perrot was born at Lyon in 1800. In his youth he toured for several years with a travelling show in which he played characters requiring an unusual acrobatic ability, such as a monkey, Polichinel, and so forth. It was doubtless this early training which procured him the rare grace and elasticity he displayed when he later became a dancer. He had almost all the natural gifts that a dancer requires—a fiery temperament, ease and lightness of movement, and excellent muscles which gave him extraordinary powers of elevation and earned for him the nickname of *l'aérien*—but nature had betrayed him by neglecting his figure.

After studying under Vestris he made his *début* at the Opéra on June 23rd, 1830, in *Le Rossignol*. Later he danced with Taglioni in *Flore et Zéphyre*. In 1840, when visiting Naples, he fell in love with the young dancer Carlotta Grisi, whom he married. They studied, travelled and danced together. On returning to Paris the couple secured an engagement at the Renaissance, where they appeared on February 28th in *Le Zingaro*.

Gautier, in a review contributed to the *Presse*, of March 2nd, 1840, says of the dancer: "Perrot is not handsome, he is extremely ugly. From the waist upwards he has the proportions of a tenor, there is no need to say more; but, from the waist downwards, he is delightful to look at. It hardly accords with modern views to discourse on a man's physical proportions; however, we cannot keep silent regarding Perrot's legs. You must imagine that we are talking of some statue of the mime Bathyllus or of the actor Paris lately discovered during an excavation of Nero's Gardens or at Herculaneum. The foot and knee joints are unusually slender and counterbalance the somewhat feminine roundness of contour of his legs; the legs of the youth in red trunks, who breaks the symbolic wand across his knee, in Raphael's painting *The Marriage of the Virgin*, are quite in the same style. Let us add that Perrot, in a costume by Gavarni, has nothing of that feeble and inane manner which, as a rule, makes male dancers so tiresome; his success was assured before he had made a single step even; it was not difficult to recognise in the quiet agility, the perfect rhythm and the easy grace of the dancer's miming,

Perrot the aerial, Perrot the sylph, Perrot the male Taglioni."

The success of the two dancers at the Renaissance secured them a position at the Opéra. From time to time Perrot made many tours and produced a number of ballets and dances, including the celebrated *Pas de Quatre* and *Pas des Déesses* staged at London in 1845 and 1848 respectively.

In 1848 he was engaged at St. Petersburg in the capacity of dancer, and thus, though he produced many ballets, it was not until 1851 that he received the official title of *maître de ballet*, which he retained until 1860. He produced a number of ballets at St. Petersburg, such as *Esmeralda, Catherine, L'Elève des Fées, The Naiad and the Fisherman, Gazelda, Faust, Marco Bomba, Armida, La Vivandière, Le Corsaire, The Rose, The Violet, Le Diable à Quatre, Le Papillon, Eoline,* and *La Débutante.*

Charles de Boigne, in his *Petits Mémoires de l'Opéra*, 1857, gives an interesting account of Perrot's method of devising *ballabili.*[1] "When the moment of inspiration seized him, he squatted on the stage, his head between his hands. He might have been a china monkey. When the *corps de ballet* saw him seated on the ground like a tailor, they knew it would be for a long time, and so every one made themselves comfortable accordingly; some embroidered, some lunched, some read, the solo dancers had refreshments brought to them. After a long interval a certain noise was heard. It was Perrot snoring. He was awakened; the *ballabile* was finished; it had arrived with the snoring."

The success of Perrot's ballets was aided by the composer Cesare Pugni, who wrote the music for most of his ballets. Marie Taglioni, Elssler, Grisi, Cerrito, Grahn—all danced to his melodies. His first ballet had a considerable success at Milan and his next efforts made him celebrated at London and Paris. He went to St. Petersburg at the same time as Elssler.

At the end of the forties there appeared the classic dancer Huguet, the future teacher of Vazem, Sokolova,

---

[1] A dance executed by a large number of persons, such as the *corps de ballet*. The term *ballabile*, derived from the Italian *ballare*, to dance, was introduced into France and other countries by Carlo Blasis. (See Blasis (Carlo), *Notes upon Dancing*, 1847, p. 111.)

Shaposhnikova and Radina. E. Huguet made his *début* in the classic *pas de deux* in Glinka's *A Life for the Tsar*.

To replace Elssler, a young and beautiful dancer, Carlotta Grisi, was engaged from Paris. Her position was a difficult one, since she had to contend with the glorious traditions of Elssler's dancing. Nevertheless, Grisi did not withdraw. She was very young and was endowed with charming eyes and small feet. A dancer of the first rank, she had a brilliant technique; the rounded grace of her movements and the brilliancy of her *pointe* work were much praised. But she lacked the personality that distinguished Taglioni and Elssler, and often she seemed more interested in dancing purely as dancing and not as a means of expressing the theme of the ballet.

Carlotta Grisi was born at Visnida, Upper Istria, 1812. At the age of seven she was learning to dance at the Scala, Milan. After a successful *début* she appeared in different performances until she was fourteen. Then she toured with a company through Italy. While at Naples she was noticed by Perrot who, astonished by her grace and ability, promised to help her with his advice. Presently he fell in love with his pupil, married her and took his wife to Paris. She made her first appearance at the Théâtre de la Renaissance on February 28th, 1840, appearing both as singer and dancer, with Perrot, in *Le Zingaro*.

Gautier acclaimed the new dancer in the following words: "She knows how to dance, a rare quality; she has fire but not enough originality, and she lacks character; this is good, but not the best. In addition to being able to dance, she is a good singer, two accomplishments not often found in company; her voice is agile, clear, a little shrill and weak in the register, but she uses it with skill and method; it is a very pleasing voice for a dancer. A great many singers who do not dance are not nearly so able. As regards her appearance, she is not a marked Italian type, and bears little resemblance to the dark features which the name of Grisi conjures up. She has chestnut hair, fair rather than dark, comparatively regular features and, so far as one can distinguish through her make-up, a naturally rosy complexion. She is of medium height, slender, well proportioned, not too thin for a dancer; but her foot is a

GALA PERFORMANCE AT PETERHOV ON JULY 11TH, 1851
From Geirot's "Opisanie Petergofa," 1868

little too Italian, or a little too English, if you like it better."

In February, 1841, she made her *début* at the Opéra, and performed a new *pas* composed by Perrot for Donizetti's opera *La Favorita*. Of her dancing, Gautier wrote: "You must remember that charming woman who sang and danced two [*sic*] years ago at the Renaissance in *Le Zingaro*, with the inimitable Perrot. She sings no longer, but she dances marvellously. She has a vigour, lightness, suppleness and originality—obviously the product of Perrot's teaching—which places her between Elssler and Taglioni. Her success is complete and enduring. She has beauty, youth and talent—three admirable qualities."

On June 28th in the same year, she achieved a triumph in the title-rôle of *Giselle*, a new ballet by Saint-Georges, Gautier and Coralli, with music by Adolphe Adam. Gautier describes her performance thus: "Carlotta danced with a perfection, lightness, assurance, and a chaste and refined voluptuousness which places her in the first rank, between Elssler and Taglioni; her pantomime surpassed the fondest hopes, there was not a single conventional gesture, not one false movement, she was nature and artlessness personified." Grisi was appointed *première danseuse noble* and followed up her success with her appearances in *La Jolie Fille du Gand, La Péri, Le Diable à Quatre* and *Paquita*. From time to time she went abroad and likewise achieved fame, particularly in London, where, in July, 1845, she danced with Taglioni, Cerrito and Lucile Grahn in the *Pas de Quatre* composed by Perrot. In 1847 she appeared at Brussels. In 1849 she went to Berlin and thence to St. Petersburg.

At the latter capital she made her *début* on October 8th, 1850, in *Giselle*. Afterwards she danced in *L'Elève des Fées, Esmeralda* and two new ballets by Perrot: *Le Diable à Quatre* (Mazilier) and *The Naiad and the Fisherman* (Perrot). The last-named was produced for Grisi in 1851. The cast was: Grisi (*Berthe*), Andreyanova (*Countess*), Perrot (*Basket-maker*) and M. I. Petipa (*Count*). Other dancers who appeared in this ballet were Smirnova, Richard, Prikhunova, Amosova, Sokolova, Radina I and II, and Snetkova. Grisi was very business-like, and asked high

F

price for her benefits, so that when other dancers gave their benefits they used to say : " Grisi prices, please."

In 1851, five *danseuses* and five *danseurs* came to St. Petersburg from Warsaw. At their *début* they danced the mazurka, and also danced it in a ballet interlude entitled *The Village Wedding*, thus the mazurka became a great favourite with the audience. The Russian dancers learned to execute the measure and it became very fashionable.

Later, F. I. Kshesinsky came to St. Petersburg. He made his *début* at the Alexandrinsky Theatre on January 30th, 1853, in *The Naiad and the Fisherman*, and danced the Cracoviak and the Cracoviak *pas de trois* with Snetkova I and Parkatcheva.

On July 11th, 1851, which was the name day of the Grand Duchess Olga Nikolaevna, a Gala Performance was given at Peterhov in the open air. The ballet *The Naiad and the Fisherman* was produced by Perrot on a specially built platform, raised just above the surface of the water, in the lake by the Ozerky Pavillion. The naiads glided to the platform in boats shaped like shells. The natural scenery of the trees, with the addition of a few tropical plants, made a charming setting. The weather was fine and a beautiful moon shone down upon the scene.

At this time, Perrot, feeling the need for a respite from his labours, no longer took an active part in all the production, and his place was taken by the Parisian *maître de ballet* Mazilier, with whose compositions the Russian public were already familiar. His new ballets, *Vert-Vert* (1851) and *The Flemish Beauty* (October, 1852), had a doubtful success. In the first the audience liked the *pas* of three feet, performed by two male dancers dressed as one. In the Spanish *pas de manteaux*, Andreyanova and M. I. Petipa were much applauded.

Mazilier was born at Bordeaux, where he began his career as a dancer. In 1822 he came to Paris and danced first at the Théâtre de la Porte St. Martin, later he appeared at the Opéra. He was appointed *premier danseur de demi-caractère* in 1833 and *maître de ballet* in 1839. It was said of him that he could compose a ballet a day and dance every night. As a composer of dances he was very inferior to Perrot, especially in *ensembles* and *ballabili*. Charles de

Boigne declares that "Mazilier was not so bad at building up a scene, but he understood nothing of the handling of masses. He did not know how to bring them on the stage, how to get them off, or how to make them move. He struggled with himself, taxed all his ingenuity in vain; he produced nothing but a muddle." Sometimes he danced in *Paquita* and *Le Diable à Quatre*. But he remained only a year at St. Petersburg and Perrot was re-engaged. Carlotta Grisi continued to delight the public, and some other ballets were staged for her—*The Woman's War, or the Amazons of the Ninth Century* (1852) and *Gazelda, or the Gypsies* (February 12th, 1853).

On Sunday, February 22nd, 1853, a remarkable performance was given on the occasion of Andreyanova's benefit. *The Hungarian Hut* was revived for Andreyanova, and with her appeared C. Grisi, Prikhunova and Amosova, and MM. Goltz, Perrot, Frédéric, Stukolkin and others. Grisi danced the *pas de deux* with Perrot, and Andreyanova performed the Hungarian Polka with M. I. Petipa. Mario sang some *arias* from the *Barbier de Seville*. Then the second act of *Cupid and Psyche* was given. The cast was: Grisi (*Cupid*), Andreyanova (*Psyche*) and Prikhunova (*Zéphyre*).

Three rising *danseuses*, whose progress was eagerly watched by the management, were Rosa Giraud, Fleury and Yella. The best of them was Yella, a well-proportioned young girl with plain features and large eyes. She made her *début* in *Gazelda* with success. She was a good dancer and a good mime. Her acting ability showed to advantage in Perrot's new ballet *Faust*, produced in 1854, in which she played the part of Gretchen. Faust was sustained by M. I. Petipa, while Perrot took the part of Mephistopheles. This ballet achieved an extraordinary success. Among numbers specially favoured were the dances of the seven mortal sins executed by Prikhunova, Richard, Radina, Amosova II, Makarova, Nikitina and Snetkova. All danced beautifully, but Prikhunova's impersonation of Luxury was the most seductive.

At this period the principal rôles were divided among Yella, Prikhunova and Richard. Yella remained at St. Petersburg until 1856, when she went to Vienna and shortly afterwards died. Richard was not beautiful, but danced lightly and had a good technique. In after years she went to Paris and married the *maître de ballet* Mérante. She then devoted herself to teaching and conducted special classes for perfection of technique.

In September, 1854, the director, Gedeonov, was succeeded by P. S. Fedorov. In 1858, the former went to Paris, where he remained until his death in 1867.

This reign saw the outbreak of the Crimean War, and while the allies were besieging Sebastopol the Emperor died on February 18th, 1855.

At this date the ballet troupe was composed as follows: *Maître de ballet*—Jules Perrot; *Regisseur*—Marcel; *2me Regisseur*—Loginov; *Professeurs de Danse*—Jean Petipa and D. Richard; *Danseuses*—Mlles. Yella, Nevakhovicheva, Yakovleva, Z. Richard, E. Nikitina, Volkova, S. Radina, Prikhunova, Makarova, Sokolova, N. Amosova I, N. Amosova II, A. Ryukhina, Misheva, Shiryaeva, Snetkova, Korostinskaya, Kostina, Danilova, Beloutovtseva, Maksimova, Samoylova, Magnus, Gopshtok, Nikulina, Gorina, Savitskaya, Bochenkova, Fedorova, Shulgina, Gertner, E. Ryukhina, Petrova, Vasilieva, Rodionova, Godovikova, Belozerova, Pavlova, Morozova, Efremova and Surovshchikova (Petipa); *Danseurs*—MM. Johannsen, Petipa, Gyuge, Kshesinsky, Goltz, Huguet, Frédéric (Maloverne,) Lede, Pankratiev, Vanner, Artemiev, Pichaud, Stukolkin, L. I. Ivanov, Pimenov, Shambursky, Morozov, Ilyin, Popov, and Gorinovsky.

MARTHA MURAVIEVA

PART IX

UNDER ALEXANDER II.

(1855–1881)

NICHOLAS I. was succeeded by his son Alexander, a humane ruler and a true friend of reform. His foreign policy raised Russia to a high place among European nations and developed her resources. The reign of Alexander II is also notable for the rise of the *bourgeoisie* and the growth of culture among the middle classes.

During the last reign, the Russian *danseuse* had learned much from personal contact with the visiting European *virtuosi* such as Taglioni, Elssler and Grisi. By a close study of their technique and styles, gained at rehearsal and in working with them during actual performances, the Russian *danseuse* gradually acquired a degree of technique which enabled her to compete at no great disadvantage with such artists. Foreign dancers, although still encouraged to visit Russia, were no longer regarded as indispensable. The public became interested in its own dancers and thus the ballet company grew independent and self-supporting.

From August 30th, 1855, to February 26th, 1866, fifty-three performances were given, nine being benefits. During this period Fanny Cerrito, M. N. Muravieva, and Nadezhda Bogdanova made their *débuts*. Perrot produced three new ballets: *Armida*, *La Vivandière* and *La Fille de*

Marbre. The most successful of these was *Armide*, given fourteen times, in which Cerrito made her first appearance at St. Petersburg.

Fanny Cerrito was born at Naples in 1821. She made her *début* at the San Carlo Theatre, Naples, in 1835, in a ballet called *The Horoscope.* She then toured most of the Italian towns. Next she spent two years at Vienna, then left for London, where she made many appearances from 1840 onwards. In May, 1841, she danced at Her Majesty's Theatre in *Le Lac des Fées*: in June, *La Sylphide* was revived for her. Afterwards she returned to Vienna. Her two greatest ballets were *Alma* and *Ondine.* The former she first danced in London in July, 1842. The next year, she appeared at Her Majesty's in *Ondine*—composed by Perrot—produced on June 22nd; in this she danced the famous *Pas de l'Ombre.* In 1845 she took part in the celebrated *Pas de Quatre*, with Grahn, Grisi and Taglioni; and in 1846 she appeared in the *Pas des Déesses,* with Grahn and Taglioni.

A contemporary says of her: "Short of stature, and round in frame, Cerrito is an example of how grace will overcome the lack of personal elegance, how mental animation will convey vivacity and attraction to features which, in repose, are heavy and inexpressive. With a figure which would be too redundant, were it not for its extreme flexibility and abandon, Cerrito is yet a charming artiste, who has honourably earned a high popularity and deservedly retained it."[1] Her particular forte appears to have been *grands jetés* and *jetés en tournant.*

She made her *début* at Paris, in 1847, in *La Fille de Marbre*, arranged by A. de Saint-Léon; other successes were *La Vivandière* and *Le Violon du Diable.* Cerrito married Saint-Léon—the celebrated dancer and *maître de ballet*—but separated from him in 1850. In 1854 she danced in *Gemma.*

Cerrito came to St. Petersburg in 1855, but, though she had preserved her grace and daintiness, the public were reserved in their welcome to her, and, in *Armida*, paid more attention to the *débutante* Muravieva, who took the part of Cupid. Cerrito danced in many short ballets

[1] *Beauties of the Opera and Ballet,* N.D. (*circa* 1845), p. 80.

FANNY CERRITO IN "ONDINE"
From the engraving by W. H. Mote after the painting by E. Smith

such as *Le Rêve du Peintre* and *La Vivandière*, and at her benefit on February 19th, 1856, she appeared in the three-act ballet, *La Fille de Marbre*, then arranged by Perrot. She made a fine success in a Spanish dance but, achieving no further triumphs, left Russia the same year.

Muravieva, whom we have just mentioned, had completed her training at the Theatre School, her teacher being Frédéric. Although not particularly graceful, she danced easily, with lightness, firm *pointes* and a rare precision; her mimetic ability, however, was limited. In 1860 she was appointed to Moscow where she continued her success.

The Russian dancers competed brilliantly with Cerrito. For instance, Z. Richard charmed the public in *Giselle* which was often performed. Some critics wrote poems in her honour.

Prikhunova was much admired in *Le Diable à Quatre*, *The Naiad and the Fisherman*, *La Fille Mal Gardée*, and *La Vivandière*. In *Paquita*, in the second act, she showed herself a good mime and danced the Spanish *pas* with a quite Southern *élan*. She was very modest and danced whatever parts were allotted to her.

Marie Sergeyevna Petipa[1] was well received in *Le Diable à Quatre* and *Esmeralda*. She was naturally gifted with an unusual grace and an ideal *plastique*; her delightful mime gave a particular charm to her dancing. Her talents, however, did not ripen fully until later. Pleshchayev is of the opinion that if she had not married the talented *maître de ballet* M. I. Petipa, she would not have become a distinguished *ballerina*, but have remained a solo dancer; for, if he had not arranged her dances and mimed scenes with a careful regard for her abilities, she would not have become prominent. Marie Petipa was excellent at character dances and even at the beginning of her career distinguished herself in such dances as the Hornpipe, Zapateado, and so forth.

Another dancer of rare promise was N. K. Bogdanova, who made her *début* in *Giselle* on February 2nd, 1856. Nadezhda Konstantinovna Bogdanova was born at Moscow in 1836. Her father, K. Bogdanov, was a dancer in the Moscow ballet and a teacher at the Theatre School. He

[1] Her maiden name was Surovshchikova.

had intended Nadezhda to become a teacher of dancing but a happy event caused him to alter his mind. When asked to dance the Cachuca at a private children's ball at Moscow, she was shy, but, being encouraged, she began to dance. Everyone was so delighted that a collection was organised and she was given 100 r. The warmth of her reception caused her father to consider her possibilities as a dancer, but there was the question of means.

Now all the members of this family were artistic. There was another daughter, Tatiana, who promised to be a good dancer, and two sons, Alexander and Nicholas, who danced and played, one the piano, the other the violin. To obtain the needed finances, the family went, in 1848, to Yaroslav and gave a number of performances. But when all the expenses had been paid there remained only a small balance. About this time, K. Bogdanov retired on a small pension and the little company made another tour, visiting Kaluga, Tula, Kursk and Kharkov. In 1849, they left Moscow a third time, for Odessa, where they achieved success. From Odessa they went to Sebastopol, Kiev, Kharkov and, in 1850, returned to Moscow. At this time Fanny Elssler was appearing there and Nadezhda was able to dance before her. The great dancer complimented her, foretold her success, and advised her to go and study at Paris.

Full of high hopes, the family set out for Paris but, having very limited means, they organised performances at different French towns in order to pay their way. At last they arrived, and then Tatiana was taken ill. A doctor was called in and, on hearing of the family's adventures, he offered to help them. He spoke to the Princess Murat, who invited the family to dance at one of her *soirées*. Nadezhda was a success and the Princess promised to plead her cause with the director of the Opéra.

In a few days' time she received an appointment and danced before the director a mazurka, a Spanish dance, and a scene from *La Sylphide*, the last with her brother and sister. The director approved of her talent, but advised her to wait a year and continue her studies. The family consented, and when this period had elapsed

NADEZHDA BOGDANOVA

Nadezhda was promised a *début* in a *pas de deux*, and Mazilier began to rehearse her.

At this time Saint-Léon returned and took Mazilier's place, but, realising the young dancer's promise, he told her that she must not dance in a *pas* but in a ballet. For this purpose he chose *La Vivandière* and lavished every care on her training. On October 20th, 1851, Bogdanova appeared before a Parisian audience and scored a success, despite the presence of F. Cerrito and Plunkett. Saint-Léon congratulated her, told her she could dance three times more but that then she must devote all her time to studying a new ballet, *Orfa*, to be produced specially for her. Saint-Léon began to study with her, but then Cerrito returned from Spain and reappeared at the Opéra. Saint-Léon resigned and was replaced by Mazilier.

The characteristic theatrical intrigue began and as a result Cerrito received all the leading parts and Bogdanova only secondary ones. Every effort was made to lower Bogdanova in the public esteem, but she astonished everyone with her dancing and was received with enthusiasm. *Orfa*, a ballet based on an eighth-century legend, was first produced on December 29th, 1852, with Cerrito as Orfa, and Bogdanova as Voluspa.

In 1855, Bogdanova left Paris on account of the anti-Russian feeling resulting from the Crimean War. When the fall of Sebastopol was announced a Gala Performance was organised at the Opéra, but Bogdanova refused to dance and left Paris. On her way to Russia she danced at Berlin and at Warsaw, and at the beginning of 1856 the family arrived at St. Petersburg, where, as we have seen, the dancer made her *début* on February 2nd in *Giselle*.

In the same year, she danced in *Esmeralda, Gazelda,* and *Faust*; and, in 1857, in *La Débutante* and *La Sylphide*. At her benefit on January 17th she appeared in a revival of *La Débutante*. The theme is concerned with a number of *danseuses* waiting for the *maître de ballet* in the green-room of the theatre. The part of *première danseuse* was taken by Prikhunova, who displayed a delicious sense of comedy in imitating the gestures of the *maître de ballet*. The part of the *ballerina* was taken by M. S. Petipa. The ballet concludes with a *divertissement*.

In February, Bogdanova received leave of absence for four months and went abroad. She danced at Warsaw, Berlin and Paris, where she was received with flowers and verses, a form of reception much in vogue at that time.

On August 17th, a Gala Performance was held at the Bolshoy Theatre on the occasion of the marriage of H.R.H. Princess Olga of Baden with the Grand Duke Michael Nikolaevich. Bogdanova, who had now returned from abroad, danced in two scenes from *Gazelda*, and a young Moscow dancer, Praskovia Prokhorovna Lebedeva, danced with Perrot in a *Pas de Quatre*.

On September 12th, Lebedeva danced the title-rôle in *Esmeralda* and was acclaimed as a future celebrity. Although no more than eighteen at this time she displayed an unusual talent for mime.

On November 6th, the *ballerina* Ekaterina Iosifovna Fridberg made her first appearance at the Bolshoy Theatre in *Armida*. Tall, graceful and well-proportioned, she was more suited to masculine rôles. She was not much liked by Russian audiences, though nobody questioned her mimetic ability.

In December, there was another *début*; a Warsaw dancer, Mme. Kozlovskaya, appeared in *La Vivandière* and in the *divertissement* in *Le Rêve du Peintre*. She danced a mazurka with Kshesinsky, also a Hungarian dance, which were well received.

The year 1858 opened auspiciously with the production of *Le Corsaire*, a pantomime ballet, in three acts, by St. Georges and Mazilier, with music by A. Adam, which was produced by Perrot for his benefit. The parts were distributed thus: Mmes. Fridberg (*Medora*), Troitskaya (*Zulméa*), Radina (*Gulnare*), Prikhunova, Amosova I, Amosova II (*Odalisques*); and MM. Petipa (*Conrad*), Perrot (*Seyd Pasha*), Pichaud (*Isaac Lanquedem*), Frédéric (*Birbanto*), Stukolkin (*Chief Eunuch*).

The best dances were the *Pas des Eventails*, *Pas des Odalisques*, and *Scène de Seduction*, danced by Radina, who, in one of the succeeding performances, was replaced by Kosheva. The character dances by Kozlovskaya and the pupils Lyadova and Kosheva pleased the audience, but the *ballerina* Fridberg was received with reserve. The ballet was handsomely produced and had a great success; the scene of the shipwreck, designed by Roller, was highly praised.

On January 21st, Bogdanova had a benefit performance. The programme was composed of scenes from different ballets. She appeared in Act II of *Giselle* and was received with thunders of applause and showers of flowers; she was recalled fifty times and presented with a diamond star which she wore in the next item, Act II of *La Sylphide*. Muravieva had a fine success in Act II of *La Fille de Marbre*. The performance ended with a *divertissement* in which the following artistes appeared: Mme. Prikhunova (*La Sicilienne*), Mme. and M. Petipa (*La Forlana*), Mlle. Lyadova and L. I. Ivanov (*Pas de Mazurka*). On this occasion Bogdanova's brother, Nicholas, took the part of James Reuben in *La Sylphide*, while in the same ballet her other brother, Alexander, played a solo on the violin.

On April 1st there was a benefit for Mme. Fridberg. She appeared as Æglia in *Cupid's Pupil* (a ballet by Taglioni), and in three scenes from *Le Corsaire*, the part of Seyd Pasha being taken by Goltz. A *divertissement*, the *pas de trois* from *The Village Wedding*, was danced by the pupils: Mlle. Alexandrova and MM. Nikitin and Paul Gerdt. Petipa witnessed the performance and prophesied a brilliant future for the last-named.

The winter season began with the production of *Robert and Bertram* and *La Vivandière*, with Mme. Prikhunova.

But everyone was eagerly awaiting the promised appearance of the celebrated Italian *danseuse* Ferraris, who had been engaged by the management, notwithstanding the presence of Mme. Fridberg.

Amalia Ferraris was born at Voghera, Piedmont, in 1830. When still a child she evinced great talent, and her teacher at Turin thought so highly of her promise, that her parents sent her to Milan to be taught by Carlo Blasis, professor at the Imperial and Royal Academy of Dancing. His school was celebrated for the talents it brought to flower; Rosati, Beretta, Baderna, Priora, Grisi, Cerrito, Fuoco, Domenichettis, Fabbri, were all his pupils. Blasis soon noted that Ferraris's talents could be used to develop the art of dancing and he taught her with assiduous care. In the autumn of 1844, while still only fourteen, she made her *début* at the Scala in the ballet *The Loves of Venus and Adonis*, in which she danced a *pas de deux* with Mérante. This was composed by Blasis himself, who wished to reveal the brilliancy of her talent. According to the description written by Regli, which appeared in the periodical *Strenna*, for 1846, " it was no more than a succession of attitudes and groups, such as may be seen in the paintings of Caracci and Albano ; the composition was intended to display distinctly the three principal characteristics of dancing, and Ferraris succeeded in them all." Her reception was favourable and she was immediately engaged for the whole season. Then she was engaged for four years at the San Carlo Theatre, Naples, where her salary was increased every year; there she created many rôles in ballets such as *La Regina delle Rose, Ondine, Fiorita, Nadilly* and *Armida*.

In 1849, during the Carnival, she danced at Turin, then at Genoa. In 1850 and 1851, she danced at Her Majesty's Theatre, London, with Carlotta Grisi. In the spring of 1852 she appeared with great success at Vienna. Then she went back to Italy and made her *début* at the Apollo Theatre, Rome, in the ballet *Ileria*; the enthusiasm was so great that she was presented with a marble bust and statuette of herself, by the sculptor Gajazzi, in the new part. At her farewell performance she was offered a golden garland bearing the words : " From the Romans to the most celebrated of dancers, the rival of Elssler." At that performance she was recalled twenty-two times. The audience wished her to stay in Rome, but she had signed a contract with the Paris Opéra, where she made her appearance on August 11th, 1856, in *Les Elfes*. The Parisian public were astonished at the lightness of her dancing and the grace of her poses and gestures, which recalled the statues of antiquity. She was regarded as one of the finest exponents of the pure Italian classic school and achieved a triumph.

On her arrival at St. Petersburg, she went to witness a ballet performance at the Bolshoy Theatre, before making her own appearance, and expressed herself delighted with the company, particularly with the solo dancers. She declared that the troupe was the best in Europe. At her

AMALIA FERRARIS IN "LES ELFES"
From the lithograph by Alophe

début in a new and final ballet by Perrot, *Eoline or The Dryad*, which took place on November 6th, 1858, the house was packed. The cast was: Ferraris (*Eoline*), M. S. Petipa (*Berta*), Lyadova II (*Trilby*), Perrot (*Rubzal*), Johannsen (*Count Edgar*), Goltz (*Duke Ratibor*), Stukolkin I (*Franz*), Pichaud (*Herman*) and Morosov I (*Servant*). Ferraris proved herself possessed of a brilliant technique and executed the most difficult *variations* with consummate ease. Her features were charming and expressive, her poses beautiful. She received a great ovation. Prikhunova, Petipa, Muravieva, Lyadova II, and Kosheva shared in her success.

Perrot's ballet *Faust* was revived for Ferraris. Her dancing was excellent, but her mime was disappointing. As Perrot had a sore foot, his place as Mephisto was taken by A. N. Bogdanov.

At the end of the year, on December 18th, M. I. Petipa produced at his benefit a little two-act ballet of his own composition entitled *Un Mariage sous la Régence*, which, although slight in theme, included some excellent dances. The best dancers, such as Prikhunova, Muravieva, M. S. Petipa and Amosova II, and Johannsen, L. Ivanov, Petipa and Stukolkin, took part in it. The dancing lessons and *pas de sept* were received with acclamation.

In 1859, the ballet was deprived of the services of the talented Perrot, who had resided in Russia for nine years; for, although his official retirement did not take place until the end of 1860, his activity ceased soon after the production of *Eoline*, owing to ill-health.

At Johannsen's benefit, *Le Diable à Quatre* was revived with Ferraris. At Fridberg's benefit, the ballet from *La Somnambule* was produced, but without success.

Owing to the illness of the principal *maître de ballet*, the repertory was restricted and Ferraris chose for her farewell benefit performance some scenes from *Giselle*, and *The Naiad*. She received a great ovation and was presented with a bracelet, ear-rings, and ring.

Fridberg went to Warsaw, where she danced in *Catherine*, *Le Corsaire*, and other ballets.

At the benefit of M. S. Petipa on April 23rd, a new one-act ballet by M. I. Petipa, *Le Marché des Innocentes*, was given; this was followed by Act II of *Le Corsaire*, in which P. P. Lebedeva danced. After this performance, both Lebedeva and Muravieva went abroad.

At the benefit of F. I. Kshesinsky, *Le Marché des Innocentes* was revived, and some dances were given in conjunction with Bulakov's choir. This scene had a great success and was performed many times, also a polka entitled " *La Rose*," danced by Kosheva, and a mazurka, called " *Laquelle des Trois*," danced by Petipa, Lyadova II and Kosheva; both these dances were arranged by Kshesinsky.

In the autumn, M. S. Petipa appeared in *Catherine*. She was very successful in character dances. At this time, Muravieva returned from abroad and appeared in Act I of *La Péri*, and danced a *pas de deux* with M. I. Petipa. She was received as an adored artist.

Then appeared two celebrities: the Italian *danseuse* Carolina Rosati, and the choreographer-violinist A. de Saint-Léon.

Carolina Rosati was born at Bologna on December 14th, 1827, and made her first stage appearance at Florence, at the age of nine, as Cupid in a mythological ballet. In 1842, she made her *début* in Venice, at the Fenice Theatre. Her grace, beauty and mimetic ability delighted the audience. She next toured a number of Italian towns, being especially successful at Rome, Turin and Milan. Rosati then went to London, where P. Taglioni composed the ballet *Coralie* for her. She also appeared at Her Majesty's Theatre, in 1848, in *Fiorita* and *Les Quatre Saisons*. She returned to Italy, where she won new successes, and passed to Paris, where she remained for four years (1854–58), during which she danced in *Le Corsaire, Les Elfes, Jovita, Esmeralda, Paquita, Giselle, La Somnambule, Marco Spada*, and others.

An anonymous writer in Larousse's *Dictionnaire du XIXe Siècle* describes her thus: " A woman of excitable nature, with a slightly satanic and somewhat mournful expression, Rosati excels in strong, noble and pathetic characters. She is no less excellent in comedy and homely parts. In the rendering of passion she is unrivalled. The most delicate gradations are rendered precisely and clearly in her miming. There is nothing vague in the expression of her thoughts and she seems to endeavour to suppress minor details, having discovered that a few chosen touches produce the most surprising effects. Her gestures are simple, her poses full of grace and harmony. . . . Ingenious, intelligent in her understanding of a character, by turns raging or tender, carried away by despair or spellbound in the ecstasy of a charming dream, she achieved by her miming the same prodigies which Ristori attained with the resources of a more complete art."

At St. Petersburg, she made her *début* in a dull ballet by Mazilier, *Jovita ou Les Boucaniers*, with music by T. Labarre, produced by Saint-Léon on September 13th (1859). She showed herself a graceful, if somewhat heavy, dancer, but a mime of the first rank. Her best dances in *Jovita* were the *pas de deux* with Johannsen, and the comic *pas* with Stukolkin; both composed by Saint-Léon. At first, she was received coldly, and it was not until the end of the performance that she attained success. The main reason for this indifference was her age. It is a curious fact that few of the European celebrities who went to Russia were in their first youth. Later, Rosati appeared in *Paquerette, Graziella, La Perle de Seville, La Fille du Pharaon, Le Corsaire*, and others. She did not prove a great attraction, although she danced at St. Petersburg for three years.

Charles Victor Arthur de Saint-Léon was born in 1815. The first ballet arranged by him was *La Fille de Marbre*, which he produced in 1847 for F. Cerrito. He composed a number of ballets for the Grand Opéra, Paris, and also wrote a treatise on a new method of dance notation which he had devised—*La Stenochorégraphie*, published 1852. He made his *début* at St. Petersburg on October 7th, 1859, in *Saltarella*, a very diverse ballet composed by himself. He was a talented mime, a dancer of a good school and a violinist, but during this performance he played the violin for so long that many spectators became drowsy.

At Johannsen's benefit, *Eoline* was revived with Prikhunova, who continued to be much admired. M. S. Petipa, who was absent, was replaced by Amosova II.

The season of 1860 was begun by the production of a number of old ballets, or scenes taken from them. Some dancers were replaced by others. Kosheva danced frequently at the Alexandrinsky Theatre. At nearly every performance a *divertissement* was given in which many principal dancers appeared.

On January 26th, 1860, at Rosati's benefit, *Paquerette*, a ballet in three acts by Saint-Léon, was produced in Russia for the first time. It contained many dances. In the first act there was an allegorical *divertissement* lasting over an hour. The dances for the *ballerina* were tedious, though effectively produced. The best numbers were those executed by M. S. Petipa, who had a fine success in "*Le Tambour de la Reine*." Rosati was inimitable in two scenes, while Stukolkin amused the audience in the character of Ignace. *Paquerette* had a long run and many Russian dancers afterwards appeared in it.

On April 12th,[1] M. I. Petipa produced a new ballet in two acts, entitled *The Blue Dahlia*, which he composed for his wife. Though slight in theme, it contained a number of beautiful dances and groups, such as: "*La Guirlande des Fleurs,*" with L. Ivanov and Lyadova II; and "*Le Dahlia Fantastique*" with M. S. Petipa. M. I. Petipa himself danced the "*Scène Dansante*" with A. D. Kosheva.

During the autumn, N. K. Bogdanova danced more frequently than the other *danseuses*, but only old ballets were produced.

On Sunday, October 2nd (1860), the new Maryinsky Theatre was opened, but on the 20th the Imperial Theatres were closed for six weeks, on account of the death of the Empress Alexandra Fedorovna, the wife of Alexander II.

In the same month, Muravieva and Frédéric went to Moscow; the first as dancer, the second as *maître de ballet*.

On December 11th, *Graziella, or a Lover's Quarrel*, a new *demi-caractère* ballet by Saint-Léon, was produced. It was a succession of scenes and dances without a theme, and not very well arranged. Both Rosati and Saint-Léon took part in it. Later on, it was condensed into one act.

At the end of the year, Lyadova II danced in *La Fille Mal Gardée*, and was much liked.

[1] D. I. Leshkov (in his *Marius Petipa*, Petrograd, 1922) gives the date as April 30th.

CAROLINA ROSATI IN "LE CORSAIRE"
From the lithograph by Alophe

In 1861, N. K. Bogdanova continued to dance in *Gazelda, Esmeralda, Le Rêve du Peintre* and *Giselle*; and Rosati in *Paquerette, Graziella* and so forth.

On January 24th, *La Perle de Seville*, a new ballet in three acts, by Saint-Léon, was first produced, with Rosati as Mariquita.

On February 19th, Pepita de Oliva, the *première danseuse* of the Royal Theatre, Madrid, danced *La Madrilena*, but she was so mediocre that the audience hissed her.

On the 23rd, *Le Météore*, a new ballet in three acts by Saint-Léon, was produced at the benefit of Bogdanova, who took the title-rôle.

During the summer, some small ballets, such as *Marco Bomba* and *The Millers*, were produced at the Kamennoe-Ostrovsky Theatre. M. S. Petipa went abroad with her husband. She did this two years in succession and danced at Paris and Berlin in *Le Marché des Innocentes* and *A Wilful Wife*. On her return to St. Petersburg she danced on September 10th in *Le Marché des Innocentes*.

On the 24th, Rosati came back and danced with Saint-Léon in *Graziella*, but she was received with reserve.

On January 18th, 1862, at Rosati's benefit, M. I. Petipa produced a grandiose ballet in three acts and six scenes, entitled *La Fille du Pharaon*. The theme was composed by Saint-Georges, the music by Pugni. This ballet played an important part in Petipa's career at St. Petersburg, for soon after its production he was appointed second *maître de ballet*, and when Saint-Léon left the stage he became the only one.

Now Rosati had expressed a wish that her last ballet should be produced by Petipa. She had reached the age of thirty-six and had resolved to leave St. Petersburg and retire. But the director of the theatre, A. I. Saburov, became annoyed with her and refused to produce the new ballet, although Pugni had already begun to work on the music. So Rosati, accompanied by Petipa, went to the director.

"What date will you appoint for the performance of the new ballet?" asked Petipa.

"I cannot give authority for any production, as we have no funds," replied Saburov.

G

"But, according to my contract, I must produce a new ballet," retorted Petipa.

"Tell me," said the director, "can you produce a ballet in seven or eight weeks?"

"Yes, if I do my best," was the answer.

Surprised by this answer, the director gave way. The ballet was ready in six weeks. It achieved a great success, although Rosati was not very suited to the part of Aspicia. She was excellent in the mimed scenes, but her dancing left much to be desired.

The principal parts were taken thus: Goltz (*Pharaoh*), F. Kshesinsky (*King of Nubia*), M. S. Petipa (*Ta-Hor*), Stukolkin (*Passifont*), L. Ivanov (*Fisherman*), Frédéric (*The Nile*), Kemmerer (*Fisherman's Wife*), Radina I (*Rameses*). All the dances were artistic, individual and original. The "*Grand Pas des Chasseresses*," "*Pas Fellah*," "*Pas de la Vision*" and "*Grand Pas des Fleuves*" were the most liked. This ballet became the most important one in the repertory and was performed at the benefit of Petipa, Pugni and others.

In May, M. N. Muravieva made her first appearance at the Grand Opéra, Paris, and delighted everyone with her dancing in *Giselle*. She was applauded for her lightness in the *pas* with the Wilis, but the success of the evening was her *pas de deux* with Mérante.

On October 4th, at the benefit of Goltz, M. S. Petipa performed the part of Aspicia for the first time. She was acclaimed with enthusiasm. One *balletomane* declared that Petipa was a very artful man, because he produced the ballet for Rosati and composed it for his wife. At this time there were two factions: the Petipistes and the Muravistes; both were jealous of each other.

In December, one of Saint-Léon's greatest creations was produced. This was *The Orphan Theolinda, or the Ghost of the Valley*, a fantastic ballet in three acts by Pugni. This was a triumph for Muravieva, who astonished everyone with her technique; her execution was likened to filigree work. The dances were excellent, especially a *pas de deux* with a reflection in a looking-glass (Radina I danced the reflection), the "*Pas des Lucioles*," the "*Pas Fantasque*" and the "*Finale*." In all these the *ballerina* was faultless and the Muravistes were delighted. In the "*Pas des Quatre Elements*," Prikhunova, Madaeva and Sokolova I were much applauded. The groups, however, were considered weak. The production occasioned so much expense that the management were forced to open a subscription.

On January 24th, 1863, *Le Corsaire* was revived with M. S. Petipa as Medora. The Petipistes not only applauded their idol, but presented her with gifts to the value of many thousand roubles. The winter season ended on February 10th, when Mme. Petipa went abroad; she returned in September and reappeared in *Le Corsaire*. In addition, the following ballets were given: *The Orphan Theolinda*; *La Fille du Pharaon*; the first two scenes from *Catherine*, with Radina I; *La Fille Mal Gardée*, with Kemmerer and L. Ivanov; *Giselle*; *The Naiad and the Fisherman*, with Muravieva; *Esmeralda*; and *Le Météore*, with Bogdanova.

The only important new ballet given that year was *The Beauty of Lebanon, or the Mountain Sprite*, with music by Pugni, produced by Petipa on December 12th. It contained many attractive dances, such as the "*Pas des Montagnards de Liban*," "*Marche des Minéraux*," "*Pas de la Colombe*," and "*Charmeuse*," in which Mme. Petipa delighted everyone. All these dances were composed with great taste. Petipa's reputation increased with each new production; the only reproach levelled at him was that, charmed by his wife's talent, he sometimes overlooked the claims of the other dancers.

The year 1864 began with a revival of *Paquerette* for Muravieva, and *Le Marché des Innocentes* for Kemmerer. On February 13th, at Muravieva's benefit, a new fantastic ballet by Saint-Léon, *La Fiametta*, with music by Minkus, was given. This had been produced before, but under another title—*The Salamander*. Muravieva took the principal part. Despite the small cost of the production, many new stage devices were introduced, such as shadow effects with the aid of convex mirrors and electric light. Muravieva's triumph was so great that Perrin, the director of the Paris Opéra, invited her to dance there. She consented and in the summer appeared at Paris in the same ballet, repeating her Russian success. The title, however, was changed to *Néméa*, and the ballet shortened.

N. K. Bogdanova danced at her benefit in scenes from *Faust*, *Giselle*, and *The Orphan Theolinda*, but from this time her fame began to wane, partly on account of the successes of Muravieva and M. S. Petipa, and partly because her abilities had begun to decline.

During May, Stukolkin broke his leg and M. S. Petipa became ill.

At Muravieva's benefit on December 3rd, a new ballet by Saint-Léon, *The Hump-backed Horse (Koniok Gorbunok)*, was produced. This was the first ballet to be based on a Russian theme. The part of the Tsar Maiden was Muravieva's last creation. Her *pirouettes* and *pointe* work left nothing to be desired. The success of the whole ballet was complete. Amosova, Efremova and Johannsen danced the " *Grand Pas*." The dances of the tribes were " *Russian Dance* " (Goltz), " *Little Russian Dance* " (Lyadova II, Sokolova II, and Bogdanov), " *Ural Dance*," (Kosheva and L. Ivanov), and others. The part of Ivan the Fool, originally created by Stukolkin, was, in consequence of his accident, taken by Troitsky. *The Hump-backed Horse* became one of the most popular of ballets and was given at St. Petersburg for over two hundred times; even to-day it still figures in the repertory.

As a result of this production, Saint-Léon became so interested in the Russian language that he began to study it and afterwards came to speak it fluently. Unfortunately, his example of planning a ballet on a Russian theme—instead of, according to custom, on a French fairy tale—was not followed.

Stukolkin returned to the stage on January 26th, 1865, and was received with long applause.

Muravieva, who had also been ill, appeared on February 8th, at the benefit for Roller and Pugni, in *The Hump-backed Horse*, but she became ill again and, on February 10th, at the benefit for the *corps de ballet*, the part of the Tsar Maiden was taken by M. N. Madaeva. This dancer was much admired by the *balletomanes*. At the last performance before Easter the part was again taken by Muravieva; a little later she retired from the stage.

MARIUS PETIPA IN "LA FILLE DU PHARAON"

From April 12th to 21st, there were no performances on account of the mourning for the death of the Tsarevich Nicholas Alexandrovich, the brother of Alexander III.

On April 25th, Madaeva again took the part of the Tsar Maiden and from that time the rôle was considered to be hers.

On September 28th, P. P. Lebedeva reappeared in *La Fiametta*; she had been engaged to take Muravieva's place. She was both an excellent classic dancer and a fine mime, and was known as the Daughter of Moscow.

The year 1865 was an unlucky one for *prime ballerine*, nearly all of whom were taken ill. Even Lebedeva did not escape and consequently she did not dance until December, when she appeared in *Paqueretta*, which was revived at the benefit of A. N. Bogdanov. Saint-Léon altered some of the scenes to provide her with an opportunity to display her mimetic ability. She achieved a considerable success, especially in the *pas de caractère* called " *La Bas Bretonne*," and the " *Grande Scène Dansante*."

At the end of the year, the pupils of the Theatre School appeared in a small ballet, *La Flûte Enchantée*, arranged by Bogdanov.

In January (1866), Lebedeva took over Muravieva's part in *The Orphan Theolinda*. She was admired, but her technique was not equal to that of her predecessor.

On January 26th,[1] a new three-act ballet was produced, *Florida*, arranged by Petipa, with music by Pugni. It was more in the nature of a *divertissement* and had been primarily designed to enable M. S. Petipa to show her versatility. She danced " *La Saltarella*," " *Peasant Dance*," " *Pavane*," " *Ecossais*," and acted a mimed scene entitled " *La Tragédie*." Kosheva distinguished herself in " *Zingara*," and Kemmerer in " *La Devineresse*." The cards for this scene of fortune-telling were the most interesting part of the ballet.

At Johannsen's benefit on the 27th, the pupils of the Theatre School again appeared in *La Flûte Enchantée*, and Kemmerer danced in the first act of *Giselle*.

On April 7th, the ballet *Catherine* was revived for the *première danseuse* of the Imperial Theatre, Vienna—Claudia Cucchi. Though her master, Blasis, regarded her as a

[1] Leshkov, *op cit.*, gives the date as January 20th.

dancer of the first rank, she was received coldly. She had an unusual technique, but lacked beauty and grace, and, moreover, was not a good mime. On the 19th, she appeared in *Esmeralda*, where her lack of mimetic ability showed to great disadvantage; but her technique was excellent, especially in a *pas de deux* with Johannsen. She later appeared with him in " *Le Carnaval de Venise*," but her reception was so indifferent that she left Russia soon afterwards.

This year marked the twenty-fifth anniversary of Johannsen's appearance on the stage and the occasion was celebrated by the artistes of the ballet company's presenting him with a gold crown, while his dressing-room was decorated with flowers and with the names of the twenty-five *ballerine* who had danced with him: Taglioni, Schlefocht, Andreyanova, Grahn, Smirnova, Yakovleva, Nikitina, Elssler, Grisi, Fleury, Giraud, Yella, Cerrito, Richard, Prikhunova, M. S. Petipa, Ferraris, Bogdanova, Fridberg, Rosati, Amosova I, Muravieva, Madaeva, Lebedeva and Cucchi.

On September 18th, a Gala Performance was given at the Bolshoy Theatre. The programme included Act I of *L'Africaine*, with Italian singers, and Act II of *La Fiametta*, with prominent Russian dancers.

A month later, Petipa revived the ballet *Satanella*, by Mazilier and Saint-Georges. Lebedeva danced very well in the " *Pas de Seduction* " and " *Le Carnaval de Venise* "; Radina I danced the *Mazurka* with Kshesinsky; and Madaeva and Gerdt had a success in a *pas de deux*.

An important event took place on December 13th at the Bolshoy Theatre, when Grantsova came from Moscow to make her *début* at St. Petersburg, in *Giselle*. Her elaborate technique, her lightness, the grace and quickness of her movements, the strength of her *pointes* caused her to be acclaimed as an ideal dancer.

Adele Grantsova was born in 1843 at Brunswick. She was taught dancing by her father, the *maître de ballet* of the local theatre. She made her *début* at the King's Theatre, Hanover, as Helen in the opera *Robert le Diable*. At this same theatre, she danced the rôle of the Dumb Girl in *Fenella*, and appeared in *Theolinda* and *Saltarella*.

In 1858, Saint-Léon, who was on leave, saw her dance. He came to the conclusion that she would be a great star and interested himself in her career. Six years later, she was engaged at Moscow, where she danced with success in *Giselle*, *La Fiametta* and *Le Météore*. In 1866, her performance of the Tsar Maiden in *The Hump-backed Horse* created a furore and resulted in her being called to St. Petersburg.

The year 1867 opened with a series of brilliant successes by Grantsova in *Le Météore* on January 17th, and in *The Hump-backed Horse* on the 29th. At her benefit on February 19th, she appeared in scenes from *La Fiametta* and the two ballets mentioned. After the " *Berceuse* " in the first-named, she was presented with a diamond star, and, at the conclusion of the performance, Goltz, on behalf of the dancers, placed a crown on her head.

Some days later, at the last performance of the season, A. N. Kemmerer was presented by the troupe with a gold *kalatch* and a fine bracelet.

Grantsova then went to Paris and appeared with success at the Grand Opéra in Saint-Léon's ballet, *La Source*. The St. Petersburg *balletomanes* sent her a telegram : " *Acceptez ce bouquet, comme faible témoignage de l'admiration profonde de vos sincères admirateurs du Nord.*"

During the spring, *The Blue Dahlia* and *La Rêve du Peintre* were revived, and E. O. Vazem and N. Alexandrova were accepted in the company.

The winter season opened on August 31st with *La Fille du Pharaon*, the part of Aspicia being taken by Kemmerer. Her dancing was excellent, but her mime inferior to that of Rosati and Petipa.

During September, Kemmerer performed the part of the Tsar Maiden in *The Hump-backed Horse*, and Ekaterina Ottovna Vazem made her *début*. The latter was a dancer of the pure classic school, possessed of a precise technique and firm *pointes*. Double *pirouettes*, which at this time were regarded as dangerous, she executed with ease.

On September 26th, the Italian *danseuse* Wilhelmina Salvioni appeared in *Le Poisson d'Or*, a new ballet by Saint-Léon. She was a pupil of Hus and made her *début* at the Scala in 1864. Two years later she danced at Paris in Rota's *Les Nuits Venitiennes*, and in *La Source*. As a mime she was reminiscent of Rosati, but her technique did not equal that of Grantsova. She attained a success in some *temps de pointe*; the ballet, however, was not much liked.

On October 17th, 1867, Vergina, the pupil of Huguet, made her *début* at the Bolshoy Theatre in *Satanella*. She was a pretty, graceful dancer, with fair hair and dark eyes, more vivacious than Vazem, but inferior to her in technical ability.

The day following there was a Gala Performance, at which Salvioni danced in some scenes from *Le Poisson d'Or*.

On January 2nd, 1868, the ballet *Faust* was revived for Salvioni; her mimed scenes were excellent and surpassed the recollections of Bogdanova and M. S. Petipa. Salvioni danced for the last time at St. Petersburg on November 21st in *Le Poisson d'Or*, when her part was taken by A. N. Kemmerer.

On November 26th, Vazem appeared with great success in *Theolinda*.

At the end of the year, Grantsova returned from Paris and danced at St. Petersburg in *Le Météore*; she was greeted with a veritable shower of flowers. A little later she appeared in *The Hump-backed Horse* and received a great ovation.

Early in 1868, Johannsen's benefit took place, when Grantsova danced in *La Fiametta*, and Vazem executed the *adage* from *Jovita*.

At Grantsova's benefit the beneficiary took the part of Medora in *Le Corsaire*. This was created in Paris by Rosati and Cucchi, and in Russia by Fridberg. Grantsova had already danced this part in Paris in 1867, when the ballet was produced under the personal direction of Mazilier. She was much applauded for her technique and mime; and when she appeared in " *Le Jardin Animé* " she performed wonders. During the performance she was presented with a tiara and two bracelets. At her farewell performance, Grantsova appeared in *The Hump-backed Horse*; on this occasion she received over three hundred bouquets.

The most talented of the younger Russian dancers were Vazem and Vergina. The former appeared at Troitsky's benefit in *Le Corsaire*, and pleased everyone with the style and finish of her dancing. Petipa composed a difficult *variation* for her, entitled " *Pas des Eventails*," containing

CHARLES V. A. DE SAINT-LÉON

double *pirouettes* and *pirouettes sur la pointe*, which she executed irreproachably. Vergina appeared at Pichaud's benefit, in *Faust*, and danced and mimed the part of Marguerite with much grace and tenderness.

But the success of the national dancers did not inspire the management to discontinue inviting foreign dancers to appear at St. Petersburg. On September 3rd, Henriette d'Or took the part of Medora in *Le Corsaire*. Her technique was not equal to Grantsova's, but she gave a very dramatic performance which greatly impressed the audience. She introduced several new *variations* into the ballet and substituted for the " *Pas des Eventails* " a difficult *pas de deux* with Johannsen, in which she astonished with her *pirouettes renversés*.

Henriette d'Or was of French descent, though born in Vienna. Her father was *premier danseur* at the Imperial Opera Theatre. Strangely enough, her mother's name was Danse. H. d'Or made her *début* at the Théâtre Royal de la Monnaie, Brussels. She then appeared with increasing success at Milan, Turin, Berlin and Paris. Just before her visit to Russia she danced at London. At all these theatres she took the principal parts in ballets by Saint-Georges or by Rota.

On October 17th, she appeared in a new grand ballet, *Le Roi Candaule*, written for d'Or by Saint-Georges and Petipa, with music by Pugni. It was produced with the greatest luxury and achieved much popularity. The sensation of the evening was the " *Pas de Venus*," in which d'Or executed a series of five *pirouettes sur la pointe* on the right foot. The ballet contained many classic dances and a number of beautiful groups. On this occasion the *ballerina* received an emerald brooch from the Tsar and a diamond tiara from the public.

On October 22nd, Evgenia Pavlovna Sokolova, a pupil of the Theatre School, made her *début*. She replaced Kemmerer I, who had gone to Moscow, in the *pas* " *Les Amours de Diane*."

On December 31st, Petipa was presented with a laurel crown on a cushion and a silver tankard ; the same evening Sokolova danced for the first time in *Le Roi Candaule*, in the *pas* entitled " *La Graciosa*."

Henriette d'Or gave her farewell performance on November 14th and then went to Moscow to dance in Petipa's production of *Le Roi Candaule*[1].

On December 5th, Grantsova reappeared in *Le Météore*, but her foot became sore, and when *The Hump-backed Horse* was produced at A. N. Bogdanov's benefit, she was replaced by Vazem.

In January, 1869, the celebrated ballet *Faust* was given for the hundredth time at the Bolshoy Theatre and a telegram was sent to Jules Perrot at Paris: " The artistes of the ballet troupe congratulate M. Perrot on the hundredth performance of the celebrated ballet *Faust*." On this occasion the part of Marguerite was taken by Vergina, who danced it better than formerly, for she had much improved her technique by studying with Johannsen.

Of new productions there were only two mediocre ballets arranged by Saint-Léon: *The Shepherd and the Bees*, a choregraphic idyll with Kantsevera and Radina, and *The Basilisk*, a comic theme based on a naturalist's mistaking the plume from a dragoon's helmet for a venomous reptile. Saint-Léon was so annoyed by the scathing criticism in the press that he challenged the critic of the *Peterburgsky Listok* to a duel.

On February 15th, there was a farewell benefit for M. S. Petipa, who wished to resign[2]. Her loss was much regretted.

At Troitsky's benefit in April, Vazem took the part of Medora in two scenes from *Le Corsaire*, and mimed the episode with the mutineers very vividly. E. P. Sokolova danced the second act from *La Fiametta* and delighted everyone with the beauty of her *plastique*.

During June, the following pupils of the Theatre School were admitted into the ballet company: E. P. Sokolova, M. Amosova, L. Trifonova, A. Selezneva, and others.

On August 31st, H. d'Or reappeared in *Le Roi Candaule* and was enthusiastically received, particularly in the " Pas de Venus." The critic of the *Golos* declared that as a virtuoso in technique she had no rival in Europe. At

---

[1] It was first performed at Moscow on December 22nd.
[2] She died in March, 1882, at Pyatigorsk in North Caucasia, a town celebrated for its medicinal springs.

Stukolkin's benefit on September 18th, d'Or appeared in *Le Corsaire* and " *Le Jardin Animé.*"

On October 21st, a new ballet by Saint-Léon, *The Lily*, was produced with Adele Grantsova, her first appearance after a long absence. The ballet, which was composed especially for her, was an adaptation in the Chinese manner of the Tale of the Hero and the Frog, with the addition of some scenes from *La Source*. Grantsova danced brilliantly, particularly in the second act with L. I. Ivanov. So many flowers were thrown on to the stage that frequently they had to be collected to enable the dancing to proceed. Amosova and Shaposhnikova danced their *variations* irreproachably, while Sokolova, Kantsevera, Gerdt and Bogdanov appeared to great advantage in a *pas de quatre*.

Henriette d'Or took her benefit on November 16th, when the Emperor was present and *La Fille du Pharaon* was given for the ninetieth time. She represented Aspicia as a woman who loves wildly and unrestrainedly, and, although her performance had nothing of the majesty of Rosati's rendering or of the coquetry of M. S. Petipa's interpretation, it made a considerable impression on the audience. On this occasion d'Or danced with success a Russian dance in Russian costume.

On January 18th, 1870, the celebrated composer Cesare Pugni died. He had a remarkable facility for composing ballet music and it was no vain boast when he said that he could easily compass twenty ballets in a season. He was thoughtless and careless of money, and so good-natured that he was always in need himself from helping others too generously.

As the end of the season approached, the greatest interest was aroused by the promised appearance of E. P. Sokolova in *Esmeralda*. She began to study dancing in 1858 and was admitted to the Theatre School the following year, on April 16th, at the suggestion of the director Saburov. Her first professor was L. I. Ivanov. At the age of ten, she took the part of Cupid in *La Perle de Seville*. In 1862, she received the pink dress[1] as a reward for her progress.

---

[1] The junior pupils wore brown, pink was awarded as a mark of distinction, while the white dress was the highest of all.

The next year she became ill and went abroad for a cure, and on her recovery she studied for three months with Mme. Blasis at Milan. In 1864, she received the white dress and passed into the highest class, where she studied with Huguet. In 1868, although still a pupil, she made her *début* in *Le Roi Candaule*. On June 8th, 1869, she was admitted into the ballet company with an annual salary of 800 r., and a subvention of a further 150 r.

In the autumn, the ballet season began with *The Humpbacked Horse*, when Vazem took the part of the Tsar Maiden. Next, *La Fille du Pharaon* was produced for Vergina, but, although she danced conscientiously, her performance did not find favour with the *balletomanes*. Later, she appeared with success in *Le Corsaire*.

During October, Grantsova reappeared in *Giselle*, and astonished everyone in her *pas de deux* with Gerdt, now one of the best classic dancers.

The year closed with a terrible accident on December 30th, when, at two o'clock in the afternoon, the dancer A. N. Prokofieva was severely burnt through her dress catching fire during a rehearsal. There was no doctor in the theatre and she died during the evening of the following day. All the artistes of the theatres and an immense number of the public attended the funeral.

At Grantsova's benefit on January 3rd,[1] 1871, a new ballet *Trilby*, with music by Gerber, was produced. It was based on the story of the same name by Charles Nodier, which inspired Nourrit's *scenario* for *La Sylphide*. This ballet was first produced at Moscow, when all the parts were taken by pupils of the Theatre School. At St. Petersburg those who took part, in addition to Grantsova, were Kusnetsova, Stukolkin, and the pupils Simskaya II, Pichaud and Zaytseva. Simskaya II was admirable as Trilby and showed great promise.

On January 31st there was a performance at the Bolshoy Theatre for the combined benefit of Vazem, Vergina and Gerdt. For this occasion Petipa composed an anacreontic scene entitled *The Two Stars*; in addition, some scenes from old ballets were given. Vazem was presented with

[1] Leshkov, *op. cit.*, gives the date as January 17th. The ballet was first produced at Moscow on January 25th, 1870.

EKATERINA VAZEM

a pair of diamond ear-rings and an album of photographs of herself in all her principal rôles ; Vergina received a diamond star ; and Gerdt a ring.

At the last performance of the season, when *Trilby* was given, Petipa's merits were recognised by the gift of a silver tea-service, while a similar service was presented to Radina.

The winter season began on August 16th. On the 25th, *Le Roi Candaule* was given, with Vergina as Nicia. In October, Grantsova reappeared in *Trilby*.

On November 9th, M. I. Petipa produced a new ballet, *Don Quichotte*, in 5 acts and 11 scenes,[1] with music by Minkus. It was based on the famous novel by Cervantes. The old and wealthy Gamache (Goltz) is to be married to the beautiful Kitri (Vergina), daughter of the innkeeper Lorenzo (Bogdanov). But Kitri has fallen in love with Basil (L. I. Ivanov). After various adventures the lovers are united through the aid of Don Quixote. Stukolkin was excellent as the apostle of knight-errantry, but the part of Kitri was beyond Vergina's powers, although she had a success with her double *tours* in the "*Grand Pas d'Adage.*" She was very dainty and coquettish in the "*Pas de l'Eventail*," and in a *pas* with a bouquet. Radina I was brilliant in a *Chica*, Kshesinsky and Tshislova danced a Mexican dance well, and Gerdt and Prikhunova had a success in a *pas de demi-caractère*. Some Spanish dances with a mock bull fight were executed by Simskaya II and eleven *danseuses* dressed in men's clothes. There was also a *Jota Aragonesa* danced by Kemmerer I and Madaeva. Amosova and Shaposhnikova also distinguished themselves. The theme, however, was somewhat involved and the audience became bored by it.

At Kshesinsky's benefit in December, the pupil Simskaya II took the title-rôle in *Catherine*, the first two scenes of the ballet being performed. The part, however, was beyond her capacity.

E. P. Sokolova married and did not dance for over two years.

[1] It was originally in 4 acts and 8 scenes, and was first produced at Moscow, on December 14th, 1869.

During January, 1872, at the benefit of A. N. Bogdanov, there were produced *Giselle*, Act I, with Grantsova; *The Two Stars*, with Vazem and Vergina; and an act from *La Péri*, with Stanislavskaya, who came from Moscow. She made her *début* as Cupid in *Le Roi Candaule*, and gradually progressed until she became a *ballerina*. Her work was of a good school, neat and studied. She had a success in an *adage* and in a *pas de deux* with Gerdt, but her mime was indifferent.

About this time, the Italian Opera Company produced *Fenella*, the part of the Dumb Girl being taken by Vergina, who gave a very expressive rendering of the character.

On February 22nd, a very important performance took place in celebration of the fiftieth anniversary of N. O. Goltz, then seventy-two years old. Nicholas Osipovich Goltz joined the Theatre School at the age of seven; he was a pupil of the celebrated Didelot. Though he did not leave the school until February 22nd, 1822, he was chosen to dance in many ballets, both as a soloist and as a mime. His biographer, A. P., who wrote a pamphlet, *To the Memory of the Fifty Years' Service of N. O. Goltz*, gives some very interesting statistics.[1]

During the first 22 years of his career, before he received the full pension, he performed rôles on 1,107 occasions, 727 times of which he performed rôles in 50 different ballets, for which the choregraphy was supplied by 12 different choregraphers; and on 380 occasions he danced different *pas* and character dances. Thus, on an average, he performed 50 times each season (33 times in parts and 17 in dances). He danced with Taglioni 203 times. During the same period there appeared and retired from the St. Petersburg stage 23 *prime ballerine*: Ikonina, Novitskaya, Istomina, Kolosova, Azarevicheva, Azlova, Lustich, Teleshova, Zubova, Velichkina, Shemaeva, B. Atrux, Alexis, Croisette, Novitskaya (Dur), L. Paysard, Schlefocht, Lecomte, Taglioni, Andreyanova, L. Grahn, Smirnova, and Nikitina.

During the last 28 years, he performed 1,080 times, on 847 of which he took rôles in 23 different ballets, composed

[1] Quoted Pleshchayev, *op. cit.* p. 202.

by 4 choregraphers; and on 233 occasions he danced character dances. Thus, on an average, he performed 39 times each season (30 in rôles, 9 in dances). During this period he danced with 24 *prime ballerine*: Fanny Elssler, C. Grisi, R. Giraud, Yella, M. S. Petipa, F. Cerrito, Prikhunova, N. Bogdanova, Fridberg, Ferraris, Rosati, Muravieva, Kemmerer, Lyadova, Madaeva, Lebedeva, Cucchi, Salvioni, Grantsova, Vergina, Vazem, E. P. Sokolova, Stefanskaya, and d'Or.

On the morning of the day appointed for his benefit, there arrived at his flat a deputation from the ballet troupe, headed by M. I. Petipa and Marcel, who presented him with an album. After the first act of *La Fille du Pharaon* he was received with continuous and unanimous applause, intermingled with shouts of " brava," and presented with a crown and a silver tankard, seven pounds in weight. After the dances from *A Life for the Tsar*, the ballet troupe formed a circle about Goltz, and Grantsova and Vazem crowned him with a gold crown. On March 9th, a dinner was given in his honour at which many prominent dancers were present, and many complimentary speeches were made. The menu included many dishes specially devised for the occasion, such as *Consommé à la Didelot* and *Pouding à la Goltz*.

On February 26th, E. O. Vazem had a benefit, at which *The Naiad and the Fisherman*—in which she had made her *début* in 1867—was given. She danced irreproachably the double *tours* in the " *Pas de l'Ombre*." Kemmerer gave an excellent performance as Janina.

The spring season began on April 20th with the production of two ballets, *The Two Thieves* and *The Village Wedding*, in which danced Kemmerer, Madaeva, Kosheva, and others.

Some days later, Amosova performed a rôle for the first time. It was in *Le Marché des Innocentes*. She was a very capable dancer with a good *élévation*, and her dances were unusually precise. Soon afterwards she had a great success as the Tsar Maiden in *The Hump-backed Horse*, but the dances were altered to suit her technique.

On May 30th, the 200th anniversary of the birth of Peter the Great, *Catherine* was given at the Bolshoy Theatre, with Vazem in the principal part. She had a brilliant and deserved success.

During June, the following were admitted into the troupe: Mlles. A. Simskaya and V. Zhukova, and M. Bystrov; while Mlles. M. Sokolova, Moreva, Apollonskaya, and M. Blech left the troupe. Mlle. N. Stanislavskaya was transferred to Moscow.

The winter season began on August 16th with *Le Corsaire*, Vazem taking the part of Medora.

In October, Grantsova was acclaimed in *Esmeralda*, in which a new *pas de cinq* created a furore. She danced at the benefits of Kshesinsky, Stukolkin, Goltz, and L. I. Ivanov.

On December 26th, the twenty-fifth anniversary of M. I. Petipa's appearance on the stage was celebrated. He chose *Trilby* for his benefit, the principal part being taken by Vazem. Before the performance a deputation from the ballet troupe, consisting of Goltz, Johannsen, the stage manager Marcel, and others, came to his flat. They escorted him to the theatre, where A. N. Bogdanov welcomed him with a speech and Goltz presented him with a gold crown on behalf of the artistes.

The first ballet arranged by Petipa on the St. Petersburg stage was *Un Mariage sous la Régence*, then came *Le Marché des Innocentes* and *The Blue Dahlia*, all for his wife. These were followed by *The Hump-backed Horse* and *La Fille du Pharaon*, both for Rosati. Next came *The Beauty of Lebanon*, *The Travelling Danseuse*, and *Florida*, all for his wife. Then he produced a small ballet, *L'Amour Bienfaiteur*, on the school stage, for E. Sokolova. Afterwards came *Le Roi Candaule* for d'Or, *The Two Stars* for Vazem and Vergina, and *Don Quichotte* for Vergina. He also produced ballets composed by other choreographers, such as: *Paquita*, *Somnambule* and *Satanella* (*Le Diable à Quatre*). He revived *Le Corsaire* and *Esmeralda*. He devised a great number of dances, such as "*Le Carnaval de Venise*" for Ferraris, "*Le Jardin Animé*" in *Le Corsaire* for Grantsova, "*La Chasse aux Alouettes*" for Vergina, the Spanish *pas* in *Catherine* for Kemmerer and Ivanov, the *pas de dix* in *Esmeralda*, and so on. A critic of the *Peterburgsky Gazetta* said: "Petipa's choregraphic compositions are distinguished by new ideas, much thought and gracefulness. Especially

NICHOLAS GOLTZ

charming and original were his *ballabili*, such as the Lydian *ballabile* in *Le Roi Candaule*, and the Nubian dance in *Don Quichotte*. They are choregraphic masterpieces."

Towards the end of the year, the choregraphic art sustained a great loss through the death at Moscow of Frédéric Maloverne. He came to St. Petersburg from London in 1830, and had served in the ballet under the name of Frédéric for forty-two years. He was the teacher of M. N. Muravieva.

Camargo, a new grand ballet in three acts, by Saint-Georges and Petipa, was produced at Grantsova's benefit on December 11th. It was an historical ballet with a fantastic element. The production was costly and Roller's scenery was much admired, particularly "Camargo's Boudoir" and "The Hall" in which the Court Performance took place. The cast included the following dancers: Radina I, Kemmerer, Kosheva, Prikhunova, Amosova, Simskaya II; and Goltz, Gerdt, Stukolkin, L. Ivanov and Kshesinsky.

On January 9th, 1873, the performances ceased on account of the death of the Grand Duchess Helen Pavlovna; they recommenced on the 16th.

Vazem's benefit, which took place on February 4th, was very successful. *Le Corsaire* was the ballet chosen. She was much applauded in a new "Pas d'Esclave," the *pas de six* in the second act, and in the poetic "*Jardin Animé*." Simskaya II was applauded for her execution of the "Pas de Forbans," and Amosova for her rendering of the *variation* in the "Pas des Odalisques."

The management did not renew Grantsova's contract, so she took her farewell performance at a *matinée* on September 20th, the programme consisting of three scenes from *Camargo*. She amazed the audience with her technique. In one *pas*, supported by her partner Gerdt, she executed the *entrechat six de volé*. The enraptured audience applauded so enthusiastically that she had to repeat the *coda*, but this time, as Gerdt had gone, she danced it without his help; this created an unprecedented furore. After Grantsova's departure the part of Camargo was taken by Vazem.

Various interesting events took place at the close of the season which it is of interest to cite. Vazem wished to go to New York, attracted by a profitable engagement, but the management would not grant her the necessary permission, fearing that she might be drowned and the troupe left without a *ballerina*. A. F. Vergina married and soon afterwards retired from the stage. Then two Gala Performances were given at the Bolshoy Theatre; one on April 20th for the German Emperor, the programme being *La Fille du Pharaon*, with Vergina; the second on May 10th for the Shah of Persia, the programme being *Le Roi Candaule*, with Vergina. On May 16th, Vergina danced at Tsarskoe Selo in two acts from *Don Quichotte*.

On the 27th, the following pupils were admitted into the troupe: Mlles. E. Volkova, E. Vergina, A. Kuzmina, El. Sokolova, and others.

The winter season began on August 23rd with *The Hump-backed Horse*, Vazem taking the part of the Tsar Maiden; the talented A. V. Shaposhnikova also danced in the ballet.

On September 4th, the scene-designer Wagner was given a benefit, the ballet being *Camargo*, with Vazem.

On October 10th, the stage-manager Marcel died, just twenty days before the fiftieth anniversary of his association with the stage. Ivan Franzovich Marcel, the son of a French emigrant, entered the St. Petersburg Theatre School in 1809. In 1834 he was appointed assistant manager to the stage manager Didier. When Gedeonov was appointed director, Marcel was made chief stage manager, which post he retained until his death. He was a great favourite with the artistes and, though only in receipt of a moderate salary, he helped many of them in their hour of need. He died a poor man and left a wife and several children, for whose benefit a special performance was given in November.

Marcel was succeeded by A. N. Bogdanov, who was accorded a salary of 3,500 r., with a half-benefit.

In December, Huguet, the former teacher at the Theatre School, came to St. Petersburg to see his old pupils. His training had produced a number of excellent dancers, such as Vazem, Kemmerer, Prikhunova, Madaeva, Vergina, Shaposhnikova, Kantsevera and Amosova, and he received a most affectionate welcome from them.

At the end of the year a number of dancers were awarded an increase in salary and the performance fee was raised; for instance, Vazem received 25 r. instead of 5 r., Kemmerer 25 instead of 15, Shaposhnikova an additional 100 r. per annum and 5 r. extra per performance, Amosova the same; Radina I was granted a half-benefit, Prikhunova received 10 r. instead of 5, and Gerdt 15 instead of 10; forty members of the *corps de ballet* received an increase of salary.

Two *coryphées* of the Moscow troupe, L. L. Savitskaya and V. D. Malchughina, were transferred to St. Petersburg.

The year 1874 began with the forty years' Jubilee of the scenic artist, A. A. Roller. He was a talented artist, a master of perspective, but an indifferent machinist.

Vazem had a benefit on January 6th, when *Le Papillon* was produced. It was a somewhat mediocre ballet in four acts, brightened by the addition of some new dances and groups. Vazem displayed a wonderful technique in the dances of the butterflies. Petipa devised many effective *variations* for solo dances in which Prikhunova, Amosova, Shaposhnikova and Simskaya II distinguished themselves. Besides these, Petipa introduced many character dances, such as "Persian Dance," "Malabar Dance" and "Circassian Dance." The part of the Maharajah's son was taken by the pupil Nedremskaya, who afterwards became a very graceful solo dancer. The ballet was indifferently received, although it was performed many times afterwards.

On the 16th, Act III of *Le Papillon* was given on the occasion of a Gala Performance in honour of the marriage of the Grand Duchess Marie Alexandrovna. Another Gala Performance was given in honour of the visit of the Austrian Emperor; the programme consisted of the opera *La Traviata*, followed by Act II of *Le Roi Candaule*, with Simskaya II.

Radina had a benefit on February 9th, when *Le Papillon* was again given. It was the tenth anniversary of her stage career and her contract was renewed for a further three years with the unusual salary of 6,000 r. per annum, a half-benefit, 35 r. per performance and three months' leave each year.

In March, an Examination Performance was held in the

Theatre School, when Act II of *La Fiametta* was given, the principal rôle being taken by the pupil Ogoleyt. Another pupil, Gorshenkova, who appeared with success in *Trilby*, at the Bolshoy Theatre, danced with the pupil Karsavin, a *pas de deux* from *Faust*, arranged by Petipa. The pupil Shaposhnikova danced the Berne dance from *Trilby*.

On April 14th, E. P. Sokolova returned to the stage with great success in Perrot's *Esmeralda*. Though she had not danced in public for over two years, she displayed an excellent technique and, as usual, charmed the audience with her grace, beauty and expressive mime.

At this period, Gustave Bournonville, the celebrated Copenhagen choreographer, a former pupil of Vestris, visited St. Petersburg.

During the summer A. Bekeffi danced at the Mineral Waters Theatre and E. Cecchetti appeared at the Egarev Garden.

The season ended with a performance of *Le Papillon* with Vazem. She had a considerable success in her *variation* on *pointes* in the third act.

Simskaya II married and shortly afterwards retired from the stage.

On August 2nd there was a Gala Performance at Tsarskoe Selo, when Acts II and III of *The Naiad and the Fisherman*, with E. P. Sokolova, were given. There was another Gala Performance at the Bolshoy Theatre on the 18th, in honour of the marriage of the Grand Duke Vladimir Alexandrovich, when two scenes from *Camargo*, with E. O. Vazem, were presented.

The performances at the Bolshoy Theatre began on the 22nd with *The Hump-backed Horse*, and Vazem as the Tsar Maiden. The part of Aspicia in *La Fille du Pharaon* was given to her, and that of Kitri in *Don Quichotte* to E. P. Sokolova. In October, the well-known dancer and *maître de ballet* of the Paris Opéra, Mérante, came to St. Petersburg to see the Imperial Ballet. He visited the Theatre School, watched the lessons and was delighted with the ballet. It will be recalled that he married the Russian *danseuse* Zina Richard, during her appearance at Paris.

Many benefits were given, the last being for Goltz, when *Camargo* was performed with the pupil Ogoleyt.

EVGENIA SOKOLOVA

Soon afterwards she appeared as Janina in *The Naiad and the Fisherman*, but her mime was not sufficiently developed.

Great interest was aroused by the benefit of P. A. Gerdt, which took place on January 12th, 1875, at the Bolshoy Theatre. *The Blue Dahlia* was given, the principal part being taken by Marie Mariusovna Petipa, the daughter of the *maître de ballet*, Petipa. The *débutante* was eighteen years old and had studied under her father's guidance. She charmed everyone with her inherited grace, daintiness, beauty and vivacity. Her dancing was marked by an unusual poetic quality which delighted the audience.

On January 26th, at the benefit of E. O. Vazem, Petipa produced a new ballet in 2 acts and 5 scenes, *The Bandits*, with music by Delibes and Minkus. The theme was simple and based on the abduction of Angela, Countess Aldini's daughter (Kusnetsova). In the prologue, the part of Angela was taken by the pupil Nedremskaya, and by Vazem in the other two acts. Ten years later, Angela is found and freed by Capt. Pepinelli (Stukolkin) and the Countess gives her consent to their marriage. The ballet concluded with a series of dances called "The Allegory of the Five Parts of the Globe." It consisted of the "March of the Five Elements," the "Dances of the Five Continents," and separate dances from different parts of the world. Vazem astonished everyone with her virtuosity. In the "*Pas de l'Enchanteresse*" she created an innovation by her endless *cabrioles*. In the classic dance "*The Fortune Teller*," her *variations* on *pointes* were ideally performed. In the scene "*Cosmopolitan Europe*," the *ballerina* showed great versatility in the different national dances, concluding with the Kamarinskaya, which she executed. Prikhunova, Kosheva, Zhukova, Glagoleva, Madaeva, Kshesinsky, Stukolkin and Troitsky appeared to advantage. In the fifth scene, Radina, Zhukova, Ogoleyt I, Gerdt, and Karsavin were applauded; and Kshesinsky and L. I. Ivanov distinguished themselves by their mime. Petipa was much praised for his charming arrangement of the dances, but criticised for their lack of connection with the theme, especially for the apotheosis, which resembled a haphazard *divertissement*.

E. P. Sokolova, whose performance fee was raised from

5 r. to 25, gave on her benefit two scenes from *Faust*, one act of *Fiametta*, and one act of *Don Quichotte*. She had her best success in the scenes from *Faust*, in which she displayed her wonderful qualities in a beautiful *pas d'action* and in a mimed scene.

The season ended with two benefits; one for L. P. Radina, the other for the *corps de ballet*. In the last-named, M. M. Petipa danced "*La Charmeuse*," which had been created by her mother.

The spring performances began on April 17th with *Le Papillon*, after which followed benefits for Troitsky and Pichaud. In *Le Papillon*, Vazem danced her *chef d'œuvre*, some *variations* to Venzano's Waltz. All the artistes were received very warmly, especially A. N. Kemmerer and L. P. Radina. The soloists, A. V. Shaposhnikova, M. I. Amosova, and A. N. Prikhunova, were distinguished by their soft movements and classic style.

During the year 1875 the following were admitted into the troupe: M. M. Petipa, A. Ogoleyt, E. Shaposhnikova, Tistrova, E. Kruger; and Platon Karsavin,[1] who aroused great hopes.

In August, when *Don Quichotte* was given, an amusing incident occurred in that Sancho Panza had to walk on foot, since it was impossible to find a donkey in the capital.

On December 14th, the pupil Gorshenkova made her *début* in *Giselle* at the benefit of A. N. Kemmerer. She was well suited to the part owing to her lightness. Her dancing showed her classic training and, although her mime was nothing out of the ordinary, she impressed the audience.

On the 31st, at the benefit of E. O. Vazem, *Le Corsaire* was given. The *ballerina* received a splendid ovation. Even in mimed scenes she carried away the audience by the thoughtfulness of her acting. The coldness which had so often hindered her success was quite absent.

On January 18th, 1876, at the benefit of E. P. Sokolova, Petipa produced *The Adventures of Peleus*, a new ballet in 3 acts and 5 scenes, with music by Delibes and Minkus. This is the theme. Peleus, during a hunt, accidentally kills King Euryation and flees to Thessaly. There he

[1] Afterwards the father of the celebrated *ballerina* Thamar Karsavina.

finds a refuge at the court of King Akastos, whose wife falls in love with him. But he repulses her and in revenge the indignant queen tells her husband that Peleus had tried to seduce her. The king commands that he be chained to a rock and left to the mercy of wild animals. But the goddess Thetis and her Nereids save him. Under the influence of Cupid, she falls in love with Peleus and brings him to Olympus, where Jupiter blesses their union.

E. P. Sokolova (Thetis) distinguished herself with Gerdt (Peleus) in "*La Danse des Nereids*" and in "*Les Transformations.*" Among the Nereids were Kemmerer, Madaeva, Shaposhnikova I, Kosheva, Prikhunova, and others. Sokolova performed with great distinction the dances "Homage to Beauty" and "The Apple of Discord," cleverly arranged on *pointes*, which had many graceful moments. The *maître de ballet* tried to adapt himself to the talents of the *ballerina* in arranging his groups. Kemmerer and Ivanov danced very well the "Infernal Dance" in the last act. In the *Bacchic Dance*, Radina I and Kshesinsky appeared. The mimed part of the Goddess of Discord was well performed by Mlle. Yartz. Petipa, who was noted for his mass effects, produced some delightful groups in the Olympus scene. The costumes and scenery, however, were not exceptional and the music was colourless and unmelodious.

In this same year there was a benefit for A. D. Kosheva in honour of her twenty-fifth anniversary on the stage. The programme consisted of scenes from different ballets. She was particularly acclaimed in a dance with a dagger from the prologue to *The Bandits*. All her dances were animated and of a remarkable rapidity, so that she resembled a spinning top. She was unrivalled in her interpretation of the mazurka. On this occasion she received a diamond bracelet with the inscription "from her fellow artistes," and a pair of ear-rings from the audience, who welcomed her with loud applause.

On February 11th, the thirtieth anniversary of the stage manager, A. N. Bogdanov's association with the stage, the artistes presented him with a silver bowl, silver bread on a tray, and a tray inscribed with the names of the subscribers to the gift.

On the 15th there was a benefit performance for the *corps de ballet*, at which *Le Roi Candaule* was given.

The year 1876 was notable in that performances were given during Lent for the first time. The repertory consisted of *Don Quichotte, Le Papillon, The Bandits, La Fille du Pharaon, The Adventures of Peleus*. First, E. A. Vazem danced and later E. P. Sokolova. On May 2nd, the performances at the Bolshoy Theatre ended. During May there were the usual examinations, and as a result Gorshenkova, Predtechina, A. Zhukova II, Gruzdovskaya, Olgina and Tsvetkova were accepted in the company.

On July 14th and 27th there were two Gala Performances at Peterhov, and one on August 7th at Tsarskoe Selo. At the first two were given Petipa's one-act ballet *A Midsummer Night's Dream* (music by Mendelssohn), and *The Two Stars*, with Sokolova and Gorshenkova. At the last-named, Act II of *Trilby* and Act II of *Peleus* were performed.

The winter season began on August 22nd with *Le Papillon*, Vazem taking the principal part.

In October, the ballet conductor A. D. Papkov was presented with a goblet on the occasion of his thirty years' service.

Sokolova was taken ill during the season and consequently Vazem had to dance at nearly every performance. She took the part of the Dumb Girl in *Fenella*, which was sung by the Italian singers, and was particularly successful in the first act.

At Vazem's benefit on January 23rd, 1877, Petipa produced *La Bayadère*, a new ballet in 4 acts and 7 scenes, with music by Minkus. The author, S. N. Khudekov, devised many dramatic scenes which provided excellent opportunities for the composition of Oriental dances and groups. Then the action was transferred to a fantastic world which afforded Petipa full scope for the introduction of many classical ballet dances.

The scene is laid in India during the Fire Festival. A Brahmin priest is to consecrate the beautiful Nikia as the Chief Bayadère, but he falls in love with her and offers her everything if she will reciprocate his passion. But she refuses his offer because she already loves the young

MATILDA MADAEVA

warrior Solor, who promises to rescue her from the Brahmin. Solor persuades Nikia to flee, which she consents to do, but makes him swear to remain true to her and foretells that if he should break faith with her a cruel punishment will befall him. The Brahmin overhears this conversation and informs the Rajah, whose daughter is betrothed to Solor. The Rajah orders Nikia to dance at the Fire Festival. Gamsatti, his daughter, calls Nikia to see if she is as beautiful as reputed. A scene of jealousy occurs between the rivals, but the Bayadère promises to dance at the festival, during which, by order of the Rajah, she is offered a basket of flowers in which a venomous snake is concealed, and she is bitten. The Brahmin offers her an antidote, but she refuses it and dies. After her death, the distraught Solor sees everywhere the shade of his beloved Bayadère. He falls asleep and in his dream visits the Kingdom of the Shades. Later he marries Gamsatti and the Bayadère's prophecy is fulfilled. There is a terrible thunderstorm and the palace falls in ruins, under which everyone is crushed to death.

The Fire Festival was admirably arranged by Petipa. There were voluptuous bayadères, fakirs flogging themselves and leaping through fire, and a number of character dances. The scene of the "Kingdom of the Shades" afforded opportunities for many beautiful *pas*, especially the *variations* for Vazem. She made a great impression in the scenes of jealousy and death. Gorshenkova danced with her usual lightness and mimed well. The ballet was enthusiastically acclaimed and attracted a great many people. At Vazem's benefit the takings with this ballet were 5,000 r., at Bogdanov's 4,600, at Radina's 4,800. At the benefit for the *corps de ballet*, the takings were 3,100 r., and on this occasion fifty-two bracelets were presented to the members of it.

When the ballet was given for Kemmerer's benefit, Petipa added a new Hindu dance called *Geni*.

On May 15th, the following pupils were admitted into the ballet troupe: Mlles. V. A. Nikitina, N. Pichaud, O. Fedorova, Z. Blech, M. Ogoleyt and others. The most talented of them was V. A. Nikitina, who, as a dancer of the first class, received a salary of 700 r.

On the 26th, the great dancer Adele Grantsova died in hospital at Berlin.

In April, there was a benefit performance for Pichaud, in honour of his forty years' service. The programme consisted of two scenes from *Useless Precautions*, with V. A. Nikitina as Lisa. She was a promising classical dancer, light in her movements, and with a dignified and poetic style, but her technique was in need of further development.

The winter season began on September 1st. First, *La Bayadère* was given; next *La Fiametta*, with Sokolova; then *Faust*, with Sokolova as Marguerite, at the benefit of Stukolkin I; afterwards *Trilby*, with Vazem, at L. I. Ivanov's benefit. There were excellent audiences at all the performances.

On January 15th, 1878, F. I. Kshesinsky had a benefit in honour of his twenty-fifth anniversary on the stage. He was born at Warsaw on November 5th, 1823, and was the son of a tenor at the Warsaw Opera House. He began to study dancing at the age of eight, under the guidance of the *maître de ballet* Pion. At the beginning of his career he devoted himself to classical ballet, but afterwards became more attached to character work and mime. In 1835 he danced at Kalisch. He did not arrive at St. Petersburg until two years later than his fellow students, owing to an injury he received during a performance of *Catherine*, when he accidentally shot his hand. Kshesinsky was renowned for his spirited dancing of the mazurka, and was even regarded as the equal of the celebrated Popel. He produced a number of ballets: *The Two Thieves*, the *Lesghinka* dances, and revived *The Village Wedding*.

On the 29th, Petipa produced a new ballet in 4 acts, *Roxana, or The Beauty of Montenegro*; theme by S. N. Khudekov, music by Minkus. The story was based on contemporary troubles in the Balkans. A Moslem living in Montenegro is in love with an orphan girl, but his passion is not reciprocated. In revenge he spreads a report that she is the cause of the troubles that have befallen the Montenegrin people, since she is in the power of her mother, who, after her death, was supposed to have become a vampire butterfly. A young Montenegrin youth, who is in love with the girl, saves her from the fury of the crowd, but learns that she is under a spell. He follows her and eventually discovers her in a fantastic wood surrounded by Wilis who, however, lose their power with the coming of dawn. He takes advantage of this fact and saves her. The vampire butterfly is killed and Roxana and the young Montenegrin are happily married.

The ballet was very successful and Petipa was recalled several times. He invested it with many picturesque touches of local colour through the use of Montenegrin dances such as the "Dance of the Eagle," the "*Kolo*," the "*Goro*," the "*Raviola*" and others, in which E. Sokolova, Radina I, Madaeva, Kemmerer, Amosova and others were well received. E. P. Sokolova had a considerable success as Roxana. Gorshenkova, Nikitina, Shaposhnikova and Prikhunova were the Wilis. Kshesinsky was very expressive as the Moslem.

On February 14th, there was a benefit for Vazem, when *Giselle* was given. But she was not suited to the part, being a dancer *terre à terre* and consequently more fitted for realistic than fantastic *rôles*.

The usual examinations took place on June 4th, and Mlles. S. Petrova, Z. Frolova, M. Simskaya and others were admitted into the troupe.

The winter season began with *La Bayadère*, the principal part being taken by E. O. Vazem.

On September 24th, there was a benefit for T. A. Stukolkin, when *Esmeralda* and *Marco Bomba* were given. At this performance, Anna Christianovna Johannsen, the daughter of the celebrated dancer and teacher, made her *début*. The influence of the Taglioni school, to which epoch her father belonged, was plainly visible in his daughter. She had an irreproachable classical style; her movements were graceful and precise, her body and legs were well placed, and she displayed an excellent *ballon*. In an *adage* with Gerdt she attracted considerable applause for her *entrechats-six*. Altogether, she made a most favourable impression.

On November 5th, Matilda Madaeva retired after twenty years' service. This graceful and talented artiste took part in every ballet from 1858 and enjoyed the constant affection of the audience. At her last benefit the programme consisted of one act each from *The Two Thieves*, *Le Poisson d'Or*, and *Camargo*, also the small ballet *The Blue Dahlia*, with Mlle. Johannsen in the principal part. In *Camargo*, Madaeva danced the "*Pas des Montagnards*" from *The Beauty of Lebanon*; and, in *Le Poisson d'Or*, a "Russian Dance" with N. O. Goltz.

E. P. Sokolova had a benefit on December 10th; the programme consisted of *The Hump-backed Horse*, in which she took the principal part with her usual grace. She was given a delightful souvenir of her rôle as the Tsar Maiden, the Daughter of the Sun and the Moon, for she was presented with diamonds set in that form.

On January 7th, 1879, there was a benefit for Vazem, when Petipa produced a new ballet in 3 acts and 5 scenes, *The Daughter of the Snows*, with music by Minkus. The first act takes place at a small sea-port in Norway, where preparations are being made for a Polar Expedition. A number of Scandinavian dances were introduced such as "*Celtringers*," the dance of the northern gypsies; "Norwegian Wedding Dance" (Kemmerer, L. Ivanov, and others); "Scandinavian Gypsy Dance" (Radina, Frolova, Kshesinsky and others). The second act depicts the hardships of the vessel and its crew amid the Land of the Snows. There were also dances of migratory birds, performed by the pupils. Then followed the appearance of the Daughter of the Snows (E. O. Vazem) in an *adage*. The act concluded with a charming "Dance of the Snowflakes." In the third act, the scene of Love and Rebirth, Nikitina was very graceful in some flower dances. The ballet was received with enthusiasm.

On the 14th, there was a Gala Performance in honour of the wedding of the Grand Duchess Anastasia Mikhaylovna; the programme consisted of three acts from *Faust*, and *Roxana*, with E. P. Sokolova.

Petipa himself seldom had a benefit performance; he preferred to receive a fixed bonus in accordance with his contract; but he made an exception that year and took a benefit on the 28th, when *The Daughter of the Snows* was given. During the performance, Petipa was presented with a silver tankard and tray.

ALEXANDRA PRIKHUNOVA

Alexandra Nikolaevna Kemmerer retired on February 25th. She had a continuous success at St. Petersburg; and at Moscow, where she danced a whole season, she took the principal parts in ballets such as *La Fille du Pharaon, Useless Precautions, Giselle, Le Poisson d'Or* and others. Kemmerer was a fine executant of mazurkas and Spanish dances. At her last performance she gave a brilliant interpretation of the title-rôle in *Giselle*.

The *corps de ballet* had a benefit on March 11th, when Petipa produced a comic ballet in one act, *Frizak or The Double Wedding*, with music by Minkus. The most popular dances were " *La Permission de Dix Heures* " (Ogoleyt); " *Pas de Deux* " (V. A. Nikitina and Karsavin); and a " Waltz," danced by a number of pupils.

On April 8th, Alexandra Ivanovna Prikhunova retired after twenty years' service. A contemporary of Madaeva and Kemmerer, she was an excellent and reliable solo dancer with a sound technique. She danced in Act I of *La Péri* and was presented with a silver shoe from the company and a brooch and ear-rings from the audience.

The season ended on April 29th with *The Daughter of the Snows*, in which Vazem obtained a real ovation; this was followed by the Ball scene from *Faust*, in which E. P. Sokolova had a great success.

On June 8th, the following pupils were admitted into the ballet: Mlles. E. Voronova, A. Fedorova, S. Andreyeva, L. Kurbanova and others.

On August 6th, Act IV of *Roxana*, with E. P. Sokolova, was given at Tsarskoe Selo.

The winter season began on the 30th; the programme consisted of Act II of *Don Quichotte*, with E. P. Sokolova; and two scenes from *Camargo*, with E. O. Vazem.

At the end of September, on the occasion of the 150th performance of *La Fille du Pharaon*, the audience presented Petipa with a large wreath bearing the figure 150.

Stukolkin I had a benefit on October 28th, when the programme consisted of *Giselle*, with Anna Johannsen as Myrta, Queen of the Wilis; and *Useless Precautions*, with E. P. Sokolova.

On November 7th, the Maly Theatre was rented by the

management. Here were given some scenes from *The Hump-backed Horse*, with Sokolova, Kshesinsky, Gerdt and Troitsky; the *pas* "*Le Carnaval de Venise*," with Vazem and Gerdt; and a " Russian Dance " by Radina and L. Ivanov.

On December 2nd, at E. P. Sokolova's benefit, Petipa produced a new ballet in 4 acts and 9 scenes, *Mlada*; theme by S. A. Gedeonov, music by Minkus. The subject is taken from the history of the Baltic Slavs in the ninth century. King Mstivoy wishes to marry his daughter Voyslava to Prince Yaromir, whose betrothed, Mlada, is poisoned to aid this plan. But Yaromir cannot forget Mlada, whose shade always follows him, and he refuses to marry Voyslava. Then the king wishes to kill him. Mlada is protected by Lada, a good genius; while Voyslava is aided by Morena, an evil genius. In the end Lada triumphs and Mlada takes Yaromir into the dwelling of the gods. There was a beautiful "*Pas d'Echarpe*" for Sokolova, and many pleasing groups. On this occasion Sokolova received a bracelet bearing the cipher X in diamonds, as it was the tenth anniversary of her appearance on the stage.

The celebrated dancer Nicholas Osipovich Goltz died on February 5th, 1880, after fifty-eight years' service.

On the 24th, the famous ballet *La Fille du Danube* was revived with new dances by Petipa, but the choregraphic art had made such progress since the days of Taglioni that the ballet appeared quite old-fashioned. Gerdt gave a wonderful rendering of the scene of madness.

On the 22nd, all the theatres were closed on account of the death of the Empress Marie Alexandrovna.

During June the following pupils were admitted into the company: Mlles. A. Vorobieva, K. Kulichevskaya, Matveyeva, Kahn, Walter, Serebrovskaya, A. Gorshenkova, Zasedateleva; also M. N. Voronkov and others.

The season began on August 30th with *La Fille du Danube*. The next day *Don Quichotte* was given. E. O. Vazem and E. P. Sokolova were well received, also Mlles. Gorshenkova, Shaposhnikova, and Amosova, and M. Gerdt. Then a number of old ballets were revived in connection with different benefit performances, such as: *La Bayadère*, with Vazem; *Graziella*, with Sokolova; *The Hump-backed*

Horse, with Sokolova, L. Ivanov and F. I. Kshesinsky; and *Le Corsaire*, with Sokolova.

On February 1st, 1881, Petipa produced a new ballet in 4 acts and 7 scenes, *Zoraiya, or The Moors in Spain*; theme by S. N. Khudekov, music by Minkus. This was given in connection with a benefit for E. O. Vazem. Soliman, the adopted son of the Khalif Abderraman, is in love with Zoraiya, the Khalif's daughter. She returns his love and has no wish to marry her father's choice, Tamarat. The jealous Tamarat spies on the lovers and endeavours to bribe some gypsies to kill Soliman. During the betrothal procession of Tamarat and Zoraiya, Soliman throws himself under the wheels of their carriage. But he recovers. He dreams of Mahomet's paradise, and sees Zoraiya as one of the houris. The dream fades and the real Zoraiya comes to visit him. She hears footsteps and hides. Tamarat enters and seeing Soliman tries to kill him, but Zoraiya comes forward. She tells everything to the Khalif, as a result of which Tamarat is dismissed and the lovers are united. The ballet contained many charming dances: "*Danse des Odalisques*" (Simskaya II, Tistrova, Kruger, Vorobieva), "*Grand Pas d'Action*" (Shaposhnikova), "*Zarandeo*" (Yartz), "*Vilano*" (Nedremskaya, Troitskaya), "*Morena*" (Amosova), "*Danse des Bedouines*" (M. M. Petipa), "*Rondeniya*" (Gorshenkova), "*Pas des Houris*" (A. Johannsen, V. A. Nikitina, Ogoleyt and Voronova) and "*Danses Abyssiniennes*" (Radina I and Manokhin). E. O. Vazem's performance as Zoraiya was much applauded. This ballet took an important place in the repertory and became a great favourite for benefit performances.

On March 1st, Alexander II was assassinated as the result of a Nihilist plot; a bomb being thrown at his carriage while he was driving past the Ekaterininsky Canal, St. Petersburg.

At the end of his reign, the ballet company was composed as follows:

Stage-manager	Bogdanov
Assistant Stage-managers	Efimov and Dyadichkin
Composer of Ballet Music	Minkus
Fencing Master	Sokolov
Maître de Ballet	M. I. Petipa

Danseurs: Akentiev, Andreyev I and II, Artemiev, Baltser, Belov, Bikov, Bistrov, Bizyukin, M. Bogdanov, N. Bogdanov, Chistyakov, Dorofeyev, Dyadichkin, Fomichev, Geltser, Genzelt, Gerdt I and II, A. Ivanov, L. Ivanov, Johannsen, Kamishev, P. Karsavin, V. Karsavin, Khamerberg, Klimashevsky, Konstantinov, Kshesinsky, Leonov, Litvinov, Lozhkin, Lukyanov, Lyusteman, Manokhin, Mikhaylov, Navatsky, Nidt, Oblakov, Orlov, Pavlov, Petrov I and II, Pichaud I and II, Puchkov, Pugni, Ryabov, Solntsev, Sprato, Stankevich, Stukolkin I and II, Tatarinov, Troitsky, Vishnevsky, Volkov, Voronin, Voronkov I and II, Yakovlev and Zelenov.

Danseuses: Aistova, Aleksandrova, N. Alekseyeva, V. Alekseyeva, Amosova, Andreyeva, Anisimova, Antonio, Artemieva, Belikhova, Blech, A. Bogdanova, M. Bogdanova, Bunyakina, Chernikova, Chistyakova, Dolganova, Egorova, Emelyanova, Fedorova, Freytag, Galkina, Glagoleva, Golubina, Gorshenkova I and II, Granken (Legat), Gruzdovskaya, Ivanova, Johannsen, Kahn, Kemmerer II, Kopp, Kruger, Kulichevskaya, Kurbanova, Kuzmina I and II, Larionova, Lelyakina, Leonova II, Lezenskaya, Litz, Lomanovskaya, Maksheyeva, Malchugina, Marzhetskaya, Matveyeva I and II, Medvedeva, Menshikova, Merzhanova, Natarova, Nedremskaya, Nesterenko, Nikitina, Nikonova, Nikulina, Niman, Novikova, Ogoleyt I, II, and III, Olgina, Olshevskaya, Palkina, Peshkova, Petipa, Petrova, Pichaud, Pimenova, Polonskaya, Potaykova, Predtechina, Prokofieva, Radina, Ribina, Sadovskaya, Savelieva, Savina, Savitskaya, Selezneva, Serebrovskaya, Shamburskaya I and II, Shukelskaya, M. Simskaya, Smirnova, El. Sokolova, E. P. Sokolova, V. Sokolova, Solovieva, Starostina, Stepanova, Tikhomirova, Tistrova, Tivolskaya, Troitskaya, Tselikhova, Tsvetkova, Ulina, Urban I and II, Usacheva, Ushakova, Vazem, L. Vishnevskaya, Voevodina, Vorobieva, Voronova, Walter, Yakovleva, Yartz, Zakrshevskaya, Zasedateleva, Zaytseva I and II, Zelenova, Zest, Zhebeleva, Zhikhareva, Zhukova I and II.

INDEX

Acts of Artaxerxes, The, 4
Adam, Adolphe, 64, 81, 90
Adam and Eve, 4
Adèle de Ponthieu, 29, 36
Adonis Transformed into a Flower, 30
Adventures of Peleus, The, 118, 120
Aeneas and Lavinia, 44
Afanasiev, 22
Afanasieva, 22
Africaine, L', 102
Aistova, 128
Akentiev, 128
Albano, 92
Alceste, 44
Aleksandrova, 128
Alekseyeva, N., 128
Alekseyeva, V., 128
Alexander I (Emperor of Russia), viii, 38, 49, 51, 52, 53
Alexander II (Emperor of Russia), 85, 96, 105, 107, 127
Alexander Compast, 29, 30
Alexandra Fedorovna (Empress of Russia), 96
Alexandrova, 31
Alexandrova, N., 91, 103
Alexeyev, 30
Alexis, 55
Alexis, Mme., 55, 110
Alexis (Tsarevich), 12
Alexis (Tsar of Moscovy), 2, 3, 4, 5, 6, 7, 13
Alma, 86
Almaviva and Rosina, 49, 55
Amadis de Gaul, 56
Amazon, The, 50
Amorous Adventures of a Boyard, The, 35
Amosova, M. I., 106, 107, 109, 111, 113, 114, 115, 118, 123, 126, 127, 128
Amosova I, N., 81, 83, 84, 90, 102
Amosova II, N., 83, 84, 90, 93, 95, 100,
Amour à la Campagne, L', 62
Amour Bienfaiteur, L', 112
Amour de Flore, L', 36
Amour Vengé, L', 30
Amours d'Automne (Les) ou les Vendangeurs, 56
Anastasia Mikhaylovna, Grand Duchess, 124
André, 45, 50, 51

Andreyanova, Elena Ivanovna, xi, 60, 62, 63, 64, 65, 66, 67, 68, 70, 74, 81, 82, 83, 102, 110
Andreyev I, 128
Andreyev II, 128
Andreyeva, S., 125, 128
Andriani, 22
Angiolini, 28, 29, 31
Anisimova, 128
Anne (Empress of Russia), 13, 14, 15, 16, 17, 18, 19
Annette and Lubim, 30
Antonen, 43, 45, 50
Antonio, 128
Antonolini, 43, 51
Antony of Brunswick-Wolfenbuttle, Prince, 18
Apollo and Daphnis (Didelot), 40
Apollo and Daphnis (Grandjé), 28
Apollo and Daphnis (Locatelli & Saccho), 22
Apollonskaya, 60, 112
Apraksina, Countess, 14
Araja, Francesco, 16, 21, 22
Argamakhov, 37
Ariadne and Bacchus, 29, 30
Armida (Grandjé), 28, 36
Armida (Perrot), 79, 85, 86, 90, 92
Arrivée de Thétis, L', 51
Artemiev, 45, 51, 52, 60, 84
Artemiev, 128
Artemieva, 128
Astarito, 43*n*
Atrux, B., 110
Attila, xiii
Atys and Galatea (Didelot), 43, 48
Atys and Galatea (Grandjé), 27, 28, 30
Auber, 56
Auguste, 30, 34, 36, 43, 45, 48, 49, 50, 51, 54, 56
Augustus II (Elector of Saxony), 14
Aventure d'une Fille de Madride, L', 69
Azarevicheva, Ekaterina, 36
Azarevicheva, Nadezhda Apollonovna, 45, 49, 51, 110
Azarova, K. P., 51
Azlova, A. T., 44, 51, 110
Baba Yaga, 14
Babini, 43
Baderna, 91
Bakst, xiii

I

Balashev, 31
Balashova, xii
Baltser, 128
Balzac, 67
Bandits, The, 117, 119, 120
Baptiste, 45, 51
Baptiste, Mlle., 44
Barbaja, 71
Barbier de Seville, 83
Barras, 34
Barrez, 68
Basilisk, The, 106
Bassevich, 9
Bayadère, La, 120, 122, 123, 126
Bayadère Amoureuse, La, 61
Bayard's Love, A, 36
Beautiful Arsena, The, 29
Beauty of Lebanon (The), or the Mountain Sprite, 99, 112, 124
Bekeffi, A., 116
Belikhova, 128
Beloutovtseva, 84
Belov, 128
Belozerova, 84
Beluzi, 22
Benningsen, Count, 37
Berchoux, 49
Beretta, 91
Berg, N. V., 74
Bergère, La, 30
Bergholz, 8
Bernadelli, M. and Mme., 45
Bertrand, Marinette, 55, 60
Bikov, 128
Birilova, Nastasia Parfentievna, 31, 35, 36, 44
Biron, 16, 17, 19
Bistrov, 128
Bizukin, 128
Blache, Alexis, 55, 56, 57, 58, 77
Blache, Jean, 56
Blasis, Carlo, x, 79*n*, 91, 92, 101
Blasis, Mme., 108
Blech, 112
Blech, Z., 121, 128
Blue Dahlia, The, 96, 103, 112, 117, 124
Bochenkova, 84
Bogdanov, Alexander K., 88, 91
Bogdanov, A. N., 93, 101, 106, 107, 109, 110, 112, 114, 119, 121, 127
Bogdanov, K., 87
Bogdanov, M., 128
Bogdanov, Nicholas K., 88, 91, 128

Bogdanova, A., 128
Bogdanova, M., 128
Bogdanova, Nadezhda Konstantinovna, 85, 87, 88, 89, 90, 91, 96, 97, 99, 100, 102, 104, 111
Bogdanova, Tatiana K., 88
Boigne, Charles de, 79, 82
Bonnat, 21
Boreas, 30
Botta, Bergonzio di, 1
Bournonville, 67, 116
Bretonne, Restif de la, 47
Bright Falcon's Feather, The, 13
Brigonzo, 23
Bruce, Countess, 14
Brunswick, Duchess of, 19
Bublikov, Timoshka, 17, 27, 28, 31
Büchner, A., 5
Bulgakov, P. A., 67
Bunyakina, 128
Burset, 43
Bystrov, 112
Caesar, 22, 28, 31
Caliph of Bagdad, The, 43, 48
Caliph of Cordova, The, 30
Camargo, 113, 114, 116, 124, 125
Camille, 50
Camp Festival, A., 51
Canziani, Joseph, 28, 29, 30, 31, 35, 51
Captive of the Caucasus, The, viii, 44, 48, 50
Caracci, 92
Caraja, 73
Caralli, xii
Carlos and Rosalba, 43, 50, 55
Carmen et son Torero, 69
Carnaval de Venise, Le, 68
Casassi, 31
Casse-Noisette, Le, xii
Castillon, 45, 50
Catherine ou la Fille du Bandit, 73, 75, 77, 79, 93, 94, 99, 101, 109, 111, 112, 122
Catherine I (Empress of Russia), 9, 10, 12, 13
Catherine II (Empress of Russia), 21, 24, 25, 26, 27, 29, 30, 31, 32, 33, 35
Cavos, Catterino, 43, 51
Cecchetti, E., vii, 116
Cerrito, Fanny, 68, 79, 81, 85, 86, 87, 89, 91, 95, 102, 111
Cervantes, 109
Charles and Lisbeth, 44, 48
Charles the Great, 27

INDEX

Charles XII (King of Sweden), 8
Chaste Joseph, The, 4
Cherkasskaya, Princess, 9
Chernikova, 128
Chetardie, Marquis de la, 20
Chevalier, 34, 35, 36
Chevalier, Mme., 34
Chinese Imperial Marriage, The, 23
Chistyakov, 128
Cianfanelli, Antonio, 31
Cleopatra's Feast, 22
Colinette, Rosa, 36, 44
Colomba, 21
Columbus, P., 31
Conoppi, 43, 52
Conquered Pirates, The, 31
Constantine, Grand Duke, 53
Constantini, Tonina, 16
Coppini, Caterina, 31
Cora and Alonzo, 44
Coralie, 94
Coralli, 64, 73, 81
Corsaire, Le, 61, 63, 79, 90, 91, 93, 94, 95, 99, 104, 105, 106, 107, 108, 112, 113, 118, 127
Cortonato, 30
Cosara, 39
Courtin, 62*n*
Croisette, 55, 110
Cucchi, Claudia, 101, 102, 104, 111
Cupid and Adonis, 49
Cupid and Psyche (Didelot), 41, 46, 49, 83
Cupid and Psyche (Le Picq) 29, 30, 31, 36
Cupid's Pupil, 91
Cupidon, 8
Danilova, 84
Danilova, Marie, 44, 45, 46, 47
Danse, 105
Danse (La), ou la Guerre des Dieux de l'Opéra, 49
Dansomanie (La) ou la Fête de M. Balloni, 56
Daphnis, 56, 57
Dauberval, ix, 28, 40
Daughter of the Snows, The, 124, 125
Débutante, La, 79, 89
Deceived Lovers, The, 36
Death of Hercules, The, 29
Delibes, 117, 118
Départ pour les Courses de Taureaux, 69
Deserter, The, 35, 49, 57

Destruction of Babylon, The, 14
Diable à Quatre, Le (Satanella), 79, 81, 83, 87, 93, 102, 104, 112
Diable Amoureux, Le, 66, 70
Diable Boiteux, Le, 71
Diaghilev, Serge de, xiii
Didelot, Charles Louis, viii, ix, xiii, 36, 39, 40, 41, 42, 43, 44, 45, 46, 47, 48, 49, 50, 51, 55, 56, 57, 62, 74, 77, 110
Didelot *fils,* 45, 51
Diderot, 28*n*
Didier, P. I., 45, 50, 51, 56, 73, 114
Dido, 44
Dido Abandoned, 28, 30
Dido and Æneas, 23
Dieu et la Bayadère, Le, 72
Djianetti, 44
Dolganova, 128
Dolgoruky, Prince, 9
Dolgorukaya, Princess, 9
Domenichettis, 91
Don Juan, 56, 57
Don Juan (Mozart), 68
Don Quichotte, 109, 112, 113, 114, 116, 118, 119, 120, 125, 126
Donizetti, 81
D'Or, Henriette, 77, 105, 106, 107, 111, 112
Dorofeyev, 128
Dostoievsky, xii
Dranchet, Louis, 52
Droit du Seigneur, Le, 69
Duncan, Isadora, xiii
Duport, Louis, viii, 45, 46, 47, 49, 50, 51
Dur, 57
Dur, Mme., *see* Novitskaya, M.D.
Dutac, 45, 49
Dya, 61
Dyadichkin, 127, 128
Ebergard, Ivan Ivanovich, 45, 50, 51, 56
Efimov, 127
Efremova, 84, 100
Egorova, 128
Ehrhard, A., 76*n*
Elève d'Amour, L', 61
Elève des Fées, L', 67, 73, 74, 79, 81
Elfes, Les, 92, 94
Elizabeth (Empress of Russia), viii, 14, 20, 22, 23, 24, 25, 35
Elssler, Fanny, 54, 67, 69, 70, 72, 73, 74, 75, 76, 77, 79, 80, 81, 85, 88, 92, 102, 111

Elssler, Jean Florian, 70
Emaux et Camées, xi
Emelyanova, 128
Engalytchev, Prince, 76
Enchanters, The, 68
Enlèvement, L', 34, 36
Eoline, 68, 79, 93, 95
Erchov, x
Ernest, 14
Esmeralda, ix, 73, 75, 77, 79, 81, 87, 89, 90, 94, 97, 99, 102, 107, 112, 116, 123
Essipov, 20n
Evgenia Onegin, 48
Fabiani, 21, 31
Fabiani, Mlle., 21
Fabbri, 91
Fabulous Comedy, The, 13
Falconet, viii, ix
Fallet, 45
False Deaf Mute, The, 29, 31
Father's Curse, The, 44
Faun and Hamadryad, 41, 43
Faust, 72, 79, 83, 89, 93, 100, 104, 105, 106, 116, 118, 122, 124, 125
Favorita, La, 81
Fedorov, 60
Fedorov, P. S., 84
Fedorova, 22
Fedorova, 84
Fedorova, A., 125, 128
Fedorova, O., 121
Fedorova, Sophie, xii
Felcht, 26
Fenella, see *Muette de Portici*
Ferraris, Amalia, 77, 91, 92, 93, 102, 111, 112
Fiametta, La, 99, 101, 102, 103, 104, 106, 116, 118, 122
Fille de Marbre, La, 86, 87, 91, 95
Fille du Danube, La, 61, 62, 68, 126
Fille du Pharaon, La, 95, 97, 98, 99, 103, 107, 108, 111, 112, 114, 116, 120, 125
Fille Mal Gardée, La, ix, 73, 75, 87, 96, 99
Fiorita, 92, 94
Flemish Beauty, The, 82
Fleur de Grènade, La, 69
Fleury, 55, 60
Fleury, Mlle., 83, 102
Flore et Zéphyre, 31, 40, 42, 43, 49, 50, 52, 55, 57, 62, 78
Florida, 101, 112
Flûte Enchantée, La, 101

Fokine, Michel, xi, xii
Fomichev, 128
Foolish Head and Kind Heart, 44
For Love of Country, 51
Frédéric, 55, 60, 83, 84, 90, 96, 98, 113
Frederick the Great (King of Prussia), 24, 33
Frederick William (Duke of Kurland), 13
Freya, 40
Freytag, 128
Fridberg, Ekaterina Iosifovna, 90, 91, 93, 102, 104, 111
Frizak or the Double Wedding, 125
Frolova, Z., 123, 124
Fuoco, 91
Furst, Otto, 10n, 13, 14
Fusi, 27, 28, 31
Fuzano, 16, 17, 20, 21
Fuzano, Julia, 16, 17, 21
Gagarin, Prince S. S., 44, 54, 55
Gagarina, Princess, 34
Gajazzi, 92
Galitsin, Prince, 75, 76
Galkina, 128
Gardel, Maximilien, 40
Gardel, Pierre, ix, 34, 42
Gaston de Foix, 34, 36
Gautier, Théophile, ix, x, 64, 71, 72, 78, 80, 81
Gavarni, 78
Gazelda, 79, 83, 89, 90, 97
Gedeonov, 57, 64, 68, 69, 70, 84, 114
Geltser, 128
Geltser, Mme., x, xii
Gemma, 86
Genzelt, 128
Georges, 44
Georges (celebrated actress), 46, 49
Gerber, 108
Gerdt, P. A., xi, 91, 102, 107, 108, 109, 110, 113, 115, 117, 123, 126, 127
Gerdt II, 128
Gerino, 57
Gerta, 61, 63
Gertner, 84
Giraud, Rosa, 83, 102, 111
Giselle, ix, 64, 68, 72, 81, 87, 89, 91, 93, 94, 97, 98, 99, 100, 101, 102, 103, 108, 110, 118, 123, 125
Gitane, La, 60, 63, 65, 68
Gladyshev, 31

INDEX

Glagoleva, 117, 128
Glazunov, xi
Glinka, 56, 80
Glushkovsky, A. P., 45
Godovikova, 84
Golden Apple at the Feasts of the Gods and the Judgment of Paris, The, 21
Golden Branch, The, 23
Golovacheva-Panaeva, A. Y., 41, 59, 64
Golóvkina, Countess, 9
Goltz, Nicholas Osipovich, 45, 50, 51, 55, 56, 60, 73, 83, 84, 91, 93, 98, 100, 103, 109, 110, 111, 112, 113, 116, 124, 126
Goltz, N. O., To the Memory of the Fifty Years Service of, 110
Golubina, 128
Gomburov, 43
Gonzago, Pietro, 31, 52
Gopshtok, 84
Gorina, 84
Gorinovsky, 84
Gorshenkova I., 116, 118, 120, 121, 123, 126, 127, 128
Gorshenkova II, A., 126, 128
Gorsky, xii
Gousse, 61
Graditious, Franz, 31
Gradzinska, Julia, 53
Grahn, Lucile, 68, 79, 81, 86, 102, 110
Grandjé, Mme., 31
Grandjé, Pierre, 27, 28, 31
Granken, 128
Grantsova, Adele, 102, 103, 104, 105, 106, 107, 108, 109, 110, 111, 112, 113, 122
Graziella, 95, 96, 97, 126
Gredlu, Emile, 58, 60, 68, 70
Gregory, Johann Gottfried, 4, 5, 6
Grekov, A., 45
Grekova, Maria, 36
Griboyedov, A. S., 48
Grimm, 28n
Grisi, Carlotta, 67, 68, 69, 77, 78, 79, 80, 81, 82, 83, 85, 91, 92, 102, 111
Grumbler, The, 39
Gruzdovskaya, 120, 128
Gugliemi, 30, 31
Guimard, Madeleine, 40
Guiseppe, 16
Gustavus III (King of Sweden), 40
Gypsies, The, 31

Gyrowetz, 73
Gyuge, 84
Happy Repentance, A, 31
Harlequin, Patron of Fairies, 30
Harrington, Lord, 13
Haydn, 71
Helen Pavlovna, Grand Duchess, 113
Henri IV, 50
Hensi and Tao, 44, 49, 55
Heroes Peace, The, 25
Hilferding, 22, 23, 27, 31
Homer, xii
Horoscope, The, 86
How Judith cut off the Head of Holofernes, 4
Hugo, Victor, ix
Huguet, E., 79, 80, 84, 104, 108, 114
Hump-backed Horse, The, 100, 103, 104, 106, 108, 111, 112, 113, 114, 116, 124, 126
Hungarian Hut, The, 43, 45, 48, 50, 57, 83
Hunting Adventure, A, 43, 48, 50, 57
Hus, 103
Ikonina, Marie Nikolaevna, 41, 44, 45, 49, 51, 110
Ileria, 92
Ilyin, 84
Intrigue Amoureuse, L', 69
Istomina, Avdotia Ilinichna, viii, 43, 44, 47, 48, 50, 110
Ivan V (Tsar of Moscovy), 7
Ivan VI, 19
Ivanov, A., 128
Ivanov, L. I., xii, 84, 91, 93, 96, 98, 99, 100, 107, 109, 112, 113, 117, 119, 122, 124, 126, 128
Ivanova, 60
Ivanova, 128
Janin, Jules, 65
Jean-Jean ou les Bonnes d'Enfants, 56
Johann George II of Wittenberg, Kürfurst, 5
Johannsen, Anna Christianovna, 123, 124, 125, 127, 128
Johannsen, Christian Petrovich, 61, 62, 67, 68, 84, 93, 95, 100, 101, 102, 104, 105, 106, 112, 128
Jolie Bordelaise, La, 69
Jolie Fille du Gand, La, 81
Joseph, Patriarch, 3n

Jovita, ou les Boucaniers, 94, 95, 104
Joyful Return of the Goddess of Spring to the Arcadian Shepherds and Shepherdesses, The, 26
Judgment of Paris, The, 49
Jugement de Paris, Le (Perrot), 68
Julia, Mme., 14
Julius Cæsar in Egypt, 55, 56
Kahn, 126, 128
Kamishev, 128
Kantemir, Princess, 9
Kantsevera, 106, 107, 114
Karatyghin, D. V., 32
Karatyghina, O. D., 31, 32
Karsavin, Platon, 116, 117, 118, 125
Karsavin, V., 128
Karsavina, Thamar, 47n, 118n
Kemmerer, Alexandra Nikolaevna, 98, 99, 101, 103, 104, 105, 109, 111, 112, 113, 114, 115, 118, 119, 121, 123, 124, 125
Kemmerer II, 128
Khamerberg, 128
Kheraskov, 26
Khitrovo,
Khovanskaya, Princess, 27
Khudekov, S. N., 120, 122, 127
Kia-King, 56
Kindhearted Gentleman, The 36
Kinsky, Count, 9
Klimashevsky, 128
Knipper, 30
Kolosova, Evgenia Ivanovna, 36, 43, 44, 45, 46, 51, 110
Kolzevaro, 22, 23
Kondratiev, 43, 52
Koni, 73
Koniok Gorbunok, see *The Humpbacked Horse*, 100
Konstantinov, 128
Kopp, 128
Korostinskaya, 84
Korovin, xii
Kosheva, A. D., 90, 93, 94, 96, 100, 101, 111, 113, 117, 119
Kozlovskaya, 90
Kostina, 84
Kotzebue, 39
Krilov, 22
Kruger, 118, 127, 128
Kshesinsky, F. I., xi, 82, 84, 90, 94, 98, 102, 109, 112, 113, 117, 119, 122, 123, 124, 126, 127
Kulichevskaya, K., 126, 128

Kunst, 10
Kurbanova, L., 125, 128
Kusnetsova, 108, 117
Kutaisov, Count, 34
Kurtasova, Theodosia, 17
Kuzmina, A., 114, 128
Kuzmina II, 128
Labarre, T., 95
Lac des Cygnes, Le, xii
Lac des Fées, Le, 61, 63, 86
Landé, 16, 17, 19, 20, 21
Lander, A. I., 51
Langage des Fleurs, La, 69
Lapukhina, 34
Larionova, 128
Larousse, 94
Lashouque, Charles, 55, 60
Laura and Henry, 41, 44
Lauretta, 30
Lauriers d'Ibérie (Les) ou la France Victorieuse, 56
Lebedeva, Praskovia Prokhorovna, 77, 90, 94, 101, 102, 111
Lebrun, Thomas, 17, 21, 23
Lecomte, 110
Lede, 84
Lefèvre, 45
Legat, xi
Lelyakina, 128
Lensky, 75
Léon, 45
Leonov, 128
Leonova II, 128
Le Picq, Charles, viii, 28, 29, 31, 34, 35, 36, 51
Le Picq, Gertrude, 29, 31, 36
Le Picq, Wilhelmine, 36
Leshkov, D. I., 96n, 101n, 108n
Lestocq, 20
Lezenskaya, 128
Liesogorov, *see* Valberg
Life for the Tsar, A, 56, 80, 111
Likhatchev, 3
Likhutina, Nathalie Andreyevna, 44, 48
Lily, The, 107
Lisa and Colin, 50
Little Hump-backed Horse, The, x
Litvinov, 128
Litz, 128
Lobanova, 44, 51
Locatelli, Giovanni, 22, 25, 26
Loduigui, Ivan, 1n
Loginov, 84
Lomanovskaya, 128
Louis XVIII (King of France), 42

Love in a Village, 56
Love is Happiness, 36
Loves of Venus and Adonis, The, 92
Lozhkin, 128
Lukyanov, 128
Lustich, 45, 50, 57
Lustich, N. A., 51, 62, 110
Lyadova, 90, 91
Lyadova II, V. A., 93, 94, 96, 100, 111
Lyusteman, 128
Madaeva, Matilda N., 99, 100, 101, 102, 109, 111, 114, 117, 119, 123, 124, 125
Madmen, The, 39
Magnanimous Pardon, A, 30
Magnus, 84
Makarova, 83, 84
Makhaeva, 44
Maksheyeva, 128
Maksimova, 84
Malchughina, V. D., 115, 128
Maloverne, Frédéric, *see* Frédéric
Mann, 10
Manokhin, 127, 128
Marcel, Ivan Franzovich, 84, 111, 112, 114
Marché des Innocentes, Le, 93, 94, 97, 99, 111, 112
Marco Bomba, 79, 97, 123
Marco Spada, 94
Maria Theresa (Empress of Austria), 20
Mariage sous le Regence, Un, 93, 112
Marie (Empress of Russia), 47
Marie Alexandrovna, Grand Duchess, 115
Marie Alexandrovna (Empress of Russia), 126
Mario, 83
Marochetti, Doctor, 58
Mars and Venus, 56
Martinov, 43, 52
Martodonis, 31
Marzhetskaya, 128
Mathieu, 60
Matveyev, Artamon Sergeyevich, 3, 4, 5, 6
Matveyeva, 126, 128
Matveyeva II, 128
Mauduit, 52
Maurer, 60
Mazilier, 67, 81, 82, 83, 89, 90, 95, 102, 104
Mecklenburg, Duchess of, 19

Medea and Jason (Didelot), 45
Medea and Jason (Le Picq), 30, 35
Medvedeva, 128
Mekeleti, 30
Menshikov, 12
Menshikova, 128
Mekeleti, 30
Mendelssohn, 120
Mérante, 84, 92, 98, 116
Mercure, 23
Mercure, Mme., 23, 31
Mercure-Prati, Mme., 31
Mercy of Titus, The, 20
Merzhanova, 128
Metamorphoses, 31
Météore, Le, 97, 99, 103, 104, 106
Meuniers, Les, 56
Michael (Tsar of Moscovy,) 1
Michael Nikolaevich, Grand Duke, 90
Midsummer Night's Dream, A, 120
Mikhaylov, 128
Mikhaylova, 22
Mikhnevich, V. O., 27
Miller, The (Auguste), 30, 35
Miller, The (Gredlu), 68
Millers, The, 97
Milon de Crotone ou les Deux Athlètes, 56
Miloradovich, Count, 47
Minerva Triumphant, 26
Minkus, 99, 109, 117, 118, 122, 124, 125, 126, 127
Misheva, 84
Mlada, 126
Montessu, 67
Mordkin, xii
Moreau, 75
Moreva, 112
Morozov, 84, 93
Morozova, 84
Mozart, 68
Muette de Portici, La, 56, 57, 68, 102, 110, 120
Murat, Princess, 88
Muravieva, Martha Nikolaevna, 74, 77, 85, 86, 87, 91, 93, 94, 96, 98, 99, 100, 101, 102, 111, 113
Nadilly, 92
Naiad and the Fisherman, The, 67, 79, 81, 82, 87, 93, 99, 111, 116, 117
Napoleon I (Emperor of France), 52
Naryshkina, Marie Antonovna, 52
Natarova, 128

Nathalie ou La Laitière Suisse, 71, 73
Nattier, A. O., 51
Navatsky, 128
Nedremskaya, 115, 117, 127, 128
Néméa, 100
Nesterenko, 128
Nesterov, Andrey, 17
Nevakhovich, 63
Nevakhovicheva, 84
New Werther, The, 35, 36
Nicholas I (Emperor of Russia), 53, 54, 59, 70, 84, 85
Nicholas Alexandrovich, Tsarevich, 101
Nidt, 128
Nijinsky, xi, xiii
Nikitin, 91
Nikitina, 44, 102, 110
Nikitina, E., 83, 84
Nikitina, V. A., 121, 122, 123, 124, 125, 127, 128
Nikonova, 128
Nikulina, 84, 128
Niman, 128
Nina, or Driven Mad by Love, 57
Noce à Nantes, La, 69
Nodier, Charles, 108
Notta, 36
Noverre, viii, 40
Novikov, xii
Novikova, 128
Nourrit, 108
Novitskaya, M. D., 56, 57, 60, 110
Novitskaya, Nastasia Semenovna, 44, 45, 47, 49, 110
Nuits Venitiennes, Les, 103
Nymphs and the Hunter, The, 36
Oblakov, 128
Œdipus, 45
Offering to Cupid, An, 36
Officer's Dance, An, with Recitative in Praise of Arms and Warriors, 8
Ogoleyt, A., 116, 117, 118, 125, 127, 128
Ogoleyt, M., 121, 128
Oiseau de Feu, L', x
Olga Nikolaevna, Grand Duchess, 82
Olga of Baden, Princess, 90
Olgina, 120, 128
Oliva, Pepita, de, 97
Olivier, 22
Olshevskaya, 128
Olympiade, 27

Ombre, L', 60
Ondine, 86, 92
Oracle, The, 29, 31, 35
Ordin-Nashchokin, Athanasius, 3
Orfa, 89
Orlov, 128
Orlov, Alexis, 25
Orlov, Gregory, 24
Orphan Theolinda (The), or the Ghost of the Valley, 98, 99, 100, 101, 102, 104
Orpheus, 5
Orpheus and Eurydice (Büchner), 5
Orpheus and Eurydice (Locatelli and Saccho), 22
Orpheus and Eurydice (Valberg), 45
Orpheus in Hades, 14
Osipova, 44
Oudinot, 75
Ovoshnikova, A. M., 44, 51
Pahlen, Count, 37
Palkina, 128
Palnikov, 51
Panin, Count, 24
Pankratiev, 84
Papillon, Le, 79, 115, 116, 118, 120
Papkov, A. D., 120
Paquerette, 95, 96, 97, 99, 101
Paquita, 66, 70, 81, 83, 94, 112
Paradise, 23, 28, 31
Parkatcheva, 82
Paris, 51
Pas de Quatre, 68, 79, 81, 86
Pas des Déesses, 68, 79, 86
Paul I (Emperor of Russia), viii, 27, 33, 35, 36, 37, 38, 53
Pavlov, 128
Pavlova, 84
Pavlova, Anna, ix
Paysard, 55, 57, 110
Peasant Festival at St. Petersburg during Carnival, A, 23
Pécourt, xiii
Péri, La, 81, 94, 110, 125
Perle de Seville, La, (Petipa), 69
Perle de Seville, La (Saint-Léon), 95, 97, 107
Perrin, 99
Perrot, Jules Joseph, ix, 67, 70, 73, 74, 77, 78, 79, 80, 81, 82, 83, 84, 85, 87, 90, 93, 106, 116
Peshkova, 128
Peter the Great (Emperor of Russia), ix, 7, 8, 9, 10, 11, 12, 13, 54, 111

Peter II (Emperor of Russia), 12, 13
Peter III (Emperor of Russia), 21, 23, 24, 25, 27
Petipa, Jean, 69, 84
Petipa, Lucien, 69
Petipa, Marie Mariusovna, 117, 118, 127
Petipa, Marie Sergeyevna, 77, 87, 89, 91, 93, 94, 95, 96, 97, 98, 99, 100, 101, 102, 103, 104, 106, 107, 111
Petipa, Marius Ivanovich, x, xii, xiii, 69, 70, 81, 82, 83, 84, 87, 90, 91, 93, 96, 97, 98, 99, 101, 104, 105, 106, 108, 109, 111, 112, 113, 115, 117, 118, 119, 120, 121, 122, 123, 124, 125, 126, 127, 128
Petite Bohémienne, La, 69
Petits Mémoires de l'Opéra, 79
Petrouchka, x, xiii
Petrov I, 128
Petrov II, 128
Petrova, 84
Petrova, S., 123, 128
Petrova, Sophia, 36
Phaedra and Hippolytus, 44, 49, 50, 55
Pichaud, 84, 90, 93, 105, 118, 128
Pichaud II, 128
Pichaud, N., 108, 121, 128
Piemontesi, 31
Pimenov, 84
Pimenova, 44
Pimenova, 128
Pinucci, 31
Pion, 122
Pitro, 31
Pleschayev, Alexis, vii, 27n, 30n, 41n, 60n, 61n, 63n, 75n, 87, 110
Pleten, Constancia, 36, 44
Plunkett, 89
Poché, 25
Poireau, Auguste, *see* Auguste
Poisson d'Or, Le, 103, 104, 124, 125
Polichinel vampire, 56
Polonskaya, 128
Popel, 122
Popov, 84
Post House at London, A, 22
Potaykova, 128
Potemkim, Prince, 28
Power of Love, The, 39
Pozharsky, 54

Predtechina, 120, 128
Premier Navigateur, Le, 40
Prince Pozharsky's Return to his Country Estate, 54
Prikhunova, Alexandra Ivanovna, 68, 81, 83, 84, 87, 89, 90, 91, 93, 95, 99, 102, 109, 111, 113, 114, 115, 117, 118, 119, 123, 125
Prior, 23
Prior, Mme., 23
Priora, 91
Prokofieva, 128
Prokofieva, A. N., 108
Psyche, 49
Puchkov, 128
Pugni, 128
Pugni, Cesare, 79, 97, 98, 100, 101, 105, 107
Pushkin, viii, 48
Puss in Boots, 98
Pyramus and Thisbe, 29
Quatre Saisons, Les, 94
Rachel, 69, 77
Radina I, 80, 81, 83, 84, 90, 98, 99, 102, 106, 109, 110, 113, 115, 117, 118, 119, 121, 123, 124, 126, 127, 128
Radina II, 81
Raikov, 39
Ramburch, Captain Stepan, 17
Raoul de Crequis, 43, 45, 48, 55
Raoul the Bluebeard, 45
Rape of Proserpine, The, 22
Raphael, 78
Razumovsky, Hetman, 24
Reconciliation of Two Brothers, The, 39
Regina delle Rose, La, 92
Regli, 92
Rejoicing of the People because Astrea has appeared on the Russian Horizon and the Golden Age has been established anew, The, 20
Return from India, The, 49
Reutova, T. S., 51, 60
Rêve du Peintre, Le, 73, 87, 90, 97, 103
Révolte du Sérail, La, 56
Ribina, 128
Riccardi, 36
Richard, D., 84
Richard, Zina, 68, 81, 83, 84, 87, 102, 116
Richard, Cœur de Lion, 40
Ristori, 77, 95

Robert and Bertram, 91
Robert le Diable, 102
Rodionova, 84
Roi Candaule, Le, 105, 106, 108, 109, 110, 112, 113, 114, 115, 120
Roland and Morgana, 41, 44
Roller, 60, 91, 100, 113, 115
Rondeau, 13
Rondeau, Lady, 14, 15, 18
Rosati, Carolina, 91, 94, 95, 96, 97, 98, 102, 104, 107, 111, 112
Rose, The, 79
Rosetti, 31
Rosière de Salency, La, 30
Rossi, Leopold Philippovich, 31, 52
Rossignol, Le, 78
Rostopchin, Countess, 76
Rota, 103, 105
Roxana, or The Beauty of Montenegro, 122, 124, 125
Rubini, 74
Ruslan and Lyudmila, 49
Russia Afflitta e Riconsollatta, La, 20
Ryabov, 128
Ryukhina, A., 84
Ryukhina, E., 84
Saburov, A. I., 97, 107
Saburova, A. T., 75
Saccho, 22
Saccho, Mme., 22
Sacre de Printemps, Le, xiii
Sadovskaya, 128
Saint-Clair, 44, 49
Saint-Georges, 81, 90, 97, 102, 105, 113
Saint-Léon, Charles Victor Arthur de, 86, 89, 94, 95, 96, 97, 98, 99, 101, 103, 106, 107
St. Stephen, Guy, 69
Salamander, The, 99, see also *Fiametta, La*
Saltarella, 95, 102
Salvioni, Wilhelmina, 103, 104, 111
Samoylova, 60, 84
Sankovskaya, E. A., 64, 66
Santini-Ubri, 23, 27, 28, 31
Satanella, see *Diable à Quatre*
Savelieva, 128
Savina, 128
Savitskaya, 84
Savitskaya, L. L., 115, 128
Scalesi, 31
Schéhérazadé, xiii

Schlefocht, Olga Timofeyevna, 55, 60, 62, 102, 110
Schmidt, see André
Schütz, Heinrich, 5
Schwabe, Jean, 31
Schwabe, Theresa, 31
Scipio, 21
Scotsmen, The, 56
Scribe, 73
Selezneva, A., 106, 128
Selezneva, U. A., 44, 51
Serebrovskaya, 126, 128
Sergeyeva, Aksinia, 17, 21, 22
Serkov, 60
Shamburskaya I, 128
Shamburskaya II, 128
Shambursky, 84
Shaposhnikova, A. V., 80, 107, 109, 114, 115, 118, 119, 123, 126, 127,
Shaposhnikova, E., 118
Shcherakova, A. V., 51
Shelekhov, 45
Shelekhov *fils*, 51
Shemaev, Ivan Antonovich, 45, 50, 51
Shemaeva, A. A., 44, 51, 110
Shenian, 60
Shepelev, 14
Shepherd and the Bees, The, 106
Shepherd's Diversion, A, 39
Sheremetev, V. V., 48
Sheremeteva, A. P., 27
Shervaieva, 51
Shipwreck and Deliverance from Ethiopian Captivity, The, 28
Shiryaeva, 60, 84
Shtellin, 20, 20n, 23
Shukelskaya,
Shulgina, 84
Simskaya, M., 123, 128
Simskaya II, 108, 109, 112, 113, 115, 116, 127
Skalkovsky, xi
Slebkin, T., 31
Sleeping Powder (A), or the Kidnapped Peasant, 39
Smirnova, 128
Smirnova, Tatiana Petrovna, 60, 62, 63, 64, 81, 102, 110
Smoltzov, xii
Snetkova I, 81, 82, 83, 84
Sobietchanska, x
Sokolov, 127
Sokolova I, 81, 84, 99
Sokolova II, 100

Sokolova, El., 114, 123, 128
Sokolova, Evgenia Pavlovna, 79, 105, 106, 107, 109, 111, 116, 117, 118, 119, 120, 122, 123, 124, 125, 126, 127, 128
Sokolova, M., 112
Sokolova, V., 128
Solich, 58
Solntsev, 128
Solomon, 39
Soloviev, N., 59n, 60n
Solovieva, 128
Somnambule, La, 68, 93, 94, 112
Sophia (Tsarevna), 7
Sosnitsky, 45
Source, La, 103, 107
Spalding, Lt.-Col., 48n
Spiridonov, 60
Spirit of Charity, The, 50
Sprato, 128
Staden, Count von, 4
Stakelberg, J., 31
Stanislavskaya, N., 110, 112
Stankevich, 128
Starostina, 128
Starzer, 23, 27
Stefanskaya, 111
Stellato, 31
Stellato, Mme., 31
Stenochorégraphie, La, 95
Stepanova, 128
Stravinsky, xiii
Striganov, G. I., 45, 51
Strugovshchikov, 14
Stukolkin, T. A., 83, 84, 90, 93, 95, 96, 98, 100, 107, 108, 109, 112, 113, 117, 122, 123, 125, 128
Stukolkin II, 128
Sumarakov, 26
Sumbeka, or the Capture of Kazan, 56
Surovshchikova (afterwards Marie Petipa), 84
Sushkov, 51
Sychev, 31
Sylphide, La, ix, xi, 56, 58, 59, 86, 88, 89, 91, 108
Swiss Milkmaid, The, 56
Sylvain ou le Braconnier, 56
Taglioni, Marie, 50, 54, 55, 58, 59, 60, 61, 62, 63, 64, 65, 68, 73, 74, 78, 79, 80, 81, 85, 86, 102, 110, 123, 126
Taglioni, Philippe, 56, 58, 73, 91, 94
Talisman and the Dancer, The, 68

Tancred, 29, 31
Tarentule, Le, 73
Tatarinov, 128
Taulato, 23, 31
Tchaikovsky, xi, xii
Télémaque, 50, 55
Teleshova, Ekaterina Alexandrovna, 44, 47, 48, 49, 51, 110
Teleshova, K. A., 56, 60
Tempête, La, 71
Temple of Joy, The, 39
Teniers, 43
Tessi, 16
Theatre Street, 47n
Théodore, 76
Theodore III (Tsar of Moscovy), 6, 7
Theodul and his Children, 39
Theseus and Ariadne, 43
Three Hunchbacks, The, 31
Thomon, Thomas de, viii, ix
Tikhomirova, 128
Timofeyeva, Avdotia, 17, 22, 31
Tistrova, 118, 127, 128
Titus, ix, 55, 56, 58, 62, 68, 69, 77
Tivolskaya, 128
Tobias, 4
Tolstoy, 12
Toporkov, Afanasy, 17, 22
Tordo, Gaetano, 21
Traitor (The), or a Woman Hero, 30
Travelling Danseuse, The, 112
Traviata, La, 115
Trifonov, N. T., 45
Trifonova, L., 106
Trilby, 108, 109, 112, 116, 120, 122
Triomphe de l'Amour, Le, 82
Triumph of Russia (The), or, The Russians in Paris, 45, 51
Troitskaya, 90, 127, 128
Troitsky, 100, 104, 106, 117, 118, 126, 128
Trubetskaya, Princess, 9
Trubetskoy, Prince, 9
Tselikhova, 128
Tshislova, 109
Tsvetkova, 120, 128
Tukmanova, 36
Turek, Franz, 52
Turek, Paul, 51
Tuscany, Duke of, 3
Two Aunts, The, 56
Two Savoyards, The, 29
Two Stars, The, 108, 110, 112, 120
Two Thieves, The, 111, 122, 124

Ulina, 128
Unexpected Return, The, 43
Urban I, 128
Urban II, 128
Urbina, 45
Usacheva, 128
Ushakova, 128
Useless Precautions, 122, 125
Valberg, I. I., 30, 31, 35, 36, 45, 49, 50, 51
Valeriani, 21, 22, 31
Valville, 43
Vanner, 84
Vanquished Prejudices, 29
Varvara, 22
Vasiliev, 22
Vasilieva, 84
Vazem, Ekaterina Ottovna, 77, 79, 103, 104, 106, 108, 110, 111, 112, 113, 114, 115, 116, 117, 118, 120, 121, 122, 123, 124, 125, 126, 127, 128
Vélange, 45, 50
Velichkina, 110
Vendange, La, 69
Venzano, 118
Vergina, A. F., 104, 105, 106, 108, 109, 110, 111, 112, 114
Vergina, E., 114
Vert-Vert, 67, 82
Vestris, Auguste, viii, xi, 28, 34, 40, 49, 78, 116
Victory of Flora over Boreas, The, 22
Village Heroine, The, 34, 36
Village Wedding, The, 82, 91, 111, 122
Violet, The, 79
Violon du Diable, Le, 86
Virgin Island, The, 56
Vishnevsky, 128
Vishnevskaya, 128
Vivandière, La, 79, 85, 86, 87, 89, 90, 91
Vladimir Alexandrovich, Grand Duke, 116
Voevodina, 128
Volbrik, Mme., 14
Volinin, xii
Volkov, T., 26, 128

Volkova, 84
Volkova, E., 114
Vorobieva, A., 126, 127, 128
Voronin, 128
Voronkov, M. N., 126
Voronkov II, 128
Voronova, E., 125, 127, 128
Vorontsova, Countess, 14
Wagner, 114
Walter, 126, 128
Wellmann, Christian Friedrich, 16
Wilful Wife, A, 67, 97
Woman's War (The), or the Amazons of the Ninth Century 83
Wooden Leg, The, 44
Yaguzhinsky, Count, 9
Yakovlev, 128
Yakovleva, 68, 84, 102, 128
Yartz, 119, 127, 128
Yella, 83, 84, 102, 111
Yeropkin, 31
Yelva ou l'Orpheline Russe, 73
Yetta, Reine des Elfrides, 61
Young Dairymaid, The, 43, 48, 55
Young Girl from the Island, The, 43, 48, 50
Young Huntress, A, 48
Zakrshevskaya, 128
Zasedateleva, 126, 128
Zaytseva, 108
Zaytseva I, 128
Zaytseva II, 128
Zelenov, 128
Zelenova, 128
Zest, 128
Zhikhareva, 128
Zhebeleva, 128
Zhukov, xii
Zhukova I, V., 112, 117, 128
Zhukova II, A., 120, 128
Zingaro, Le, 78, 80, 81
Zoraida, 56
Zoraiya, or the Moors in Spain, 127
Zorina, Elizaveta, 17
Zotov, 63
Zubov, Brothers, 37
Zubova, Vera Andreyevna, 44, 47, 48, 51, 110
Zucchi, Virginia, **73**

www.ingramcontent.com/pod-product-compliance
Lightning Source LLC
Chambersburg PA
CBHW021832110526
R18278100001B/R182781PG44588CBX00001B/1